A Practical Guide To

Bryan-College Station

Diane L. Oswald

Lacewing Press

A Practical Guide To

Bryan-College Station

Diane L. Oswald

Copyright © 1998 by Diane L. Oswald

Editor: Alma Maxwell

Printed and bound by Newman Printing, Bryan, Texas

To order additional copies of this book or to place an advertisement in future editions contact:

Lacewing Press
15889 Woodlake Drive
College Station, Texas 77845
(409) 690-7251

Oswald, Diane L.
A Practical Guide to Bryan/College Station
Diane Oswald. – First Edition
Includes Index
1. Travel Guide 2. Local Directory
ISBN 0-9659698-1-9

Table of Contents

About...

The Author

Diane L. Oswald is the author of *101 Great Collectibles for Kids* and *Fire Insurance Maps, Their History and Applications.*

With over 100 published articles, Diane's work has appeared in *Texas Magazine, Country Weekly, Business Geographics* and other regional and national publications.

Diane is a featured speaker at conferences, workshops and in classrooms.

She is President of Brazos Writers and an active member of the Brazos Valley Society of Children's Authors and Illustrators.

Diane lives in College Station, Texas with her husband, John and their two children, Emily and Scott.

See "Family Pak"
p. 60

The Illustrator

Timothy Vanya, who created the artwork for the cover, is the Artist in Residence and co-owner of the Red Brick Studios & Gallery in Historic Downtown Bryan, Texas.

Timothy works primarily in graphite and color pencil and has done commission work for Texas A&M University and the Corps of Cadets.

Timothy studied Fine Arts at the University of Houston and lives with his family in College Station, Texas.

The Photographer

Rhonda Brinkmann, who took many of the photographs included in this book, is a writer/photographer and owner of *Wordsmiths* Writing and Editing located in Historic Downtown Bryan, Texas.

Rhonda is a touring artist with the Austin Writer's League, a past President of Brazos Writers and an active member of the community.

The Publisher

A Practical Guide to Bryan-College Station is the second release for Lacewing Press. The press' first book, *Fire Insurance Maps, Their History and Applications* has been well received in academic and cartographic communities.

Lacewing Press is dedicated to publishing quality books about subjects that may have been overlooked by the larger publishing houses.

Thanks and Kudos

When my family moved to Bryan-College Station, I looked for a book that covered everything that there is to do and see here. Now, I think I know why there wasn't one – writing such a tome is a lot of work!

Trying to include every fun, interesting and useful aspect of our sprawling community was pretty daunting. I couldn't have completed this first effort without a lot of help.

To the following people go big kudos and my heartfelt thanks for their contribution: Timothy Vanya of the Red Brick Studios and Gallery for the artistic rendition of Bryan-College Station that graces the cover. Our roving photographer, Rhonda Brinkmann of Wordsmiths, did a wonderful job capturing on film some of the people and places that make our community so special. Many thanks to Alma Maxwell for her encouragement and editing skills.

Joe Brown from the City of Bryan, Don and Myra Morrison of Myra's Gallery and Custom Framing, Dick Forester and the entire staff at the Bryan-College Station Convention and Visitor's Bureau, Louis Newman and Bob Bilberry at Newman Printing and Larry Hodges of Copy Corner were early champions of this project.

Their enthusiasm and support meant the world to me!

I want to thank my friends Vicki Scott, Leann Nichols and Cathy Dean for watching my two wonderful kids so that I could keep appointments or write. I also appreciate Liz Sulak, Noel Salata, Mike Dean, and Greg Salata for mentioning a few things that may have been overlooked.

Thanks to all of our advertisers without whom this book would not have been possible. They represent some of the finest businesses that Bryan-College Station has to offer. Please shop in their stores, eat in their restaurants and use their services.

Many other people were instrumental in helping to compile the information contained in this book. However, trying to name every city employee, businessperson or resident who answered questions, sent information or provided direction would be impossible. Please accept my sincere appreciation for all of the help.

Finally, I want to say thanks to my family – John, Emily and Scott, not only for encouragement and for enduring yet another book, but also for sharing with me the wonderful things that there are to do and see in Bryan-College Station!

◆ ◆ ◆ ◆ ◆ ◆ ◆

Bryan-College Station Climate Stats

Average hours sunshine	**8 hours per day**
Average daily wind speed	**4 miles per hour**
Prevailing wind direction	**Southerly**

How to Use this Book

This book was designed to be your "owner's manual" for Bryan-College Station. It isn't a novel so you don't need to read it from cover to cover. It isn't a text book so you don't have to memorize it. Just keep it handy and refer to it as needed.

Stuff it in your backpack, throw it on the dashboard, strap it to your bike or toss it on the desk. Whether your time in our community is measured in days, semesters or years, you will find most of what you need to know about Bryan-College Station within these 112 pages.

The chapters are arranged by specific categories but there may be some overlap. A park for example, may appear in both the "Park It" and "Family Pak" chapters due to the tennis courts or swimming pool that are located there.

Photo: City of Bryan
Books – check them out at the local library!

We've tried to make the book as "user friendly" as possible. Each chapter exists independently so skip around a bit. Need something to do on a Friday night? Check out the "Night Club" chapter. Looking for a great place to have your child's birthday party? There are a dozen places detailed in the "Family Pak" chapter. Want to try a new restaurant? Turn to the "Craving Cuisine" chapter to discover some great local haunts.

Newcomers might want to review the "Overview" or "That's History" chapters. Business people may want to check out the "Just the Facts" or the "Big Business" chapters. Peruse, use and abuse this text any way you see fit!

Although we tried our level best to include only valid, current information, keep in mind that things do change. Hours, locations and prices change. Businesses sometimes close. So, call ahead to confirm when possible.

Countless hours have been spent on the telephone, driving around and talking with other residents and business owners to create a comprehensive guide. The early reports are that we have done a fine job. However, something may have been overlooked.

If there's anything that you'd like to see in the next edition, if you have comments, complaints or compliments, please drop us a note. We'd love to hear from you!

Lacewing Press, 15889 Woodlake Dr. College Station, Texas 77845.

Overview

A *Practical Guide to Bryan-College Station* is the tale of two cities and the people, places and events that make the area so enjoyably unique. The twin cities have attractions and amenities that you might expect to find in a more cosmopolitan area, yet we don't have the pollution, crime or congestion that is the bane of many large cities.

You'll find the people friendly, the cost of living reasonable and the quality of life high. As far as things to do, well, you may have some notion about what you'll find here, but there are bound to be some surprises. Like the heat in a good bowl of chili, there is more to Bryan-College Station than meets the eye.

Texas A&M University is a major contributor to Bryan-College Station's way of life. According to the state comptroller, in 1995, the University contributed approximately $168 million to the local economy. Beyond the economic impact, Texas A&M contributes greatly to the quality of life in the community it calls home.

The Aggies volunteer countless hours to various local non-profit groups. They raise funds, tutor school children and working on special projects. During A&M's "Big Event," over 4,000 students donate their time to paint houses, move dirt and wash windows for residents who need a helping hand.

The cultural events that a world-class university brings are unparalleled in other communities our

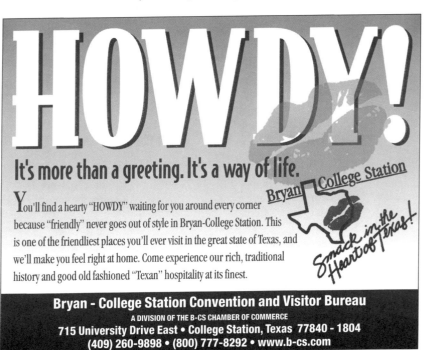

size. Art, theater and musical events are plentiful and reasonably priced.

As part of the Big Twelve, Texas A&M offers exciting football, basketball and other athletic events for sports enthusiasts.

Although often thought of as "just a college-community," Bryan-College Station is also a great place to raise children.

Students in the Bryan-College Station school districts consistently achieve TAAS scores that are above the state average and all local campuses have a rating of "Acceptable" or better.

Educational excellence is complimented by a wide variety of supplemental learning opportunities. Museums, parks and local libraries all have programs tailored to meet the needs and interests of young residents.

Bryan College Station also has a number of local attractions. An award- winning winery, a children's museum, over 50 city parks, art galleries, several distinct shopping districts, fine eateries and more will keep visitors and newcomers busy for quite a while. The entertainment options and annual events will make you wish that there were a few more hours in each day.

If you're lucky enough to live here, then a strong local economy combined with a high employment rate is probably good news. The business and industrial base is growing and becoming increasingly more diverse. Large employers such as Texas A&M University, Sanderson Farms and Universal Computer Services are joined by over 3,000 other businesses in providing ever expanding employment opportunities.

We are proud of our community and pleased to welcome you!

Getting Here and Around

Bryan-College Station is "Smack in the Heart of Texas." Approximately 80% of the State's population is located within a 200-mile radius. Austin is 90 miles to the west, Dallas is 165 miles north, Houston is 90 miles south and San Antonio is 180 miles southwest of Bryan-College Station. A web of U.S. highways, state routes and Interstate highways makes Bryan-College Station very accessible from these metropolitan cities.

By Car

Bryan-College Station is situated in the center of a triangle bounded by Interstate highways 45, 35 and 10. None of these major thoroughfares actually pass through Bryan-College Station, but they connect with the appropriate feeder highways that lead into town.

From Dallas/Ft. Worth the most direct route is I45 South to State Highway 21 into Bryan-College Station.

From Houston, take U.S. Highway 290 West to Texas Route 6 North into Bryan-College Station.

From San Antonio, take I 35 North into Austin to U.S. Highway 290 East to State Highway 21 into Bryan-College Station.

From Austin, take U.S. Highway 290 East to State Highway 21 into Bryan-College Station.

See "Maps" pp. 11 & 12

By Plane

American Eagle and Continental Express serve Bryan-College Station. Daily commuter flights depart College Station's Easterwood Airport with service to and from Dallas/Fort Worth and Houston.

The airport is about ¼ mile away from Texas A&M University and is accessible from FM 60. Most local hotels have a courtesy shuttle that transports guests to and from the airport.

American Eagle 800-433-7300
Continental Express 846-4979

By Bus

Greyhound Bus Lines serves Bryan-College Station with a depot at 405 E. 29th St. (B). The local number is 779-8071. Greyhound's toll-free number is 1-800-231-2222.

Getting Around

After arriving in Bryan-College Station, most travel takes place on

FYI

ABC Taxi 778-4000
Advantage Taxi 779-8030
University Taxi 846-2233

9

small intracity roads, state routes or state highways.

Bryan-College Station is driver friendly, streets are easy to find and "rush hour" consists of little more than a five-minute delay. The inside joke is that everything is located on Texas Avenue. Of course that isn't true, but you'll probably spend a good deal of time on this main thoroughfare. Other primary roads include the Highway 6 Bypass to the east and FM 2818 to the west, which form a mini-loop around the twin cities. Briarcrest, Villa Maria, University, George Bush Drive, and Harvey Road are major east/west arteries. See the maps at the end of this chapter to get your bearings. A more detailed map is often available at low or no cost from the Bryan-College Station Tourist Bureau and from area hotels and retailers.

Public Transportation

Bryan-College Station has an Interurban Trolley System that provides a fixed route and demand/response service within the city limits. The hours of operation are from 6 a.m. until 6 p.m. Mon. – Fri. For information call 778-0607.

Texas A&M Bus Operations runs on and off campus routes to accommodate students, faculty and staff. For more information call 845-1971.

Local taxi cab service is available and there are several rental car agencies within Bryan-College Station.

◆◆◆◆◆◆◆

Distance in Miles from B-CS

Dallas	180	Houston	93
Denver	673	Chicago	1,125
Los Angeles	1,550	New York	1,785

10

Bryan Map

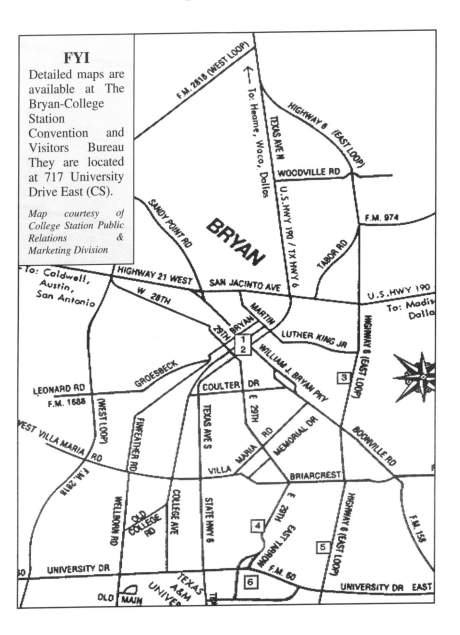

FYI

Detailed maps are available at The Bryan-College Station Convention and Visitors Bureau They are located at 717 University Drive East (CS).

Map courtesy of College Station Public Relations & Marketing Division

College Station Map

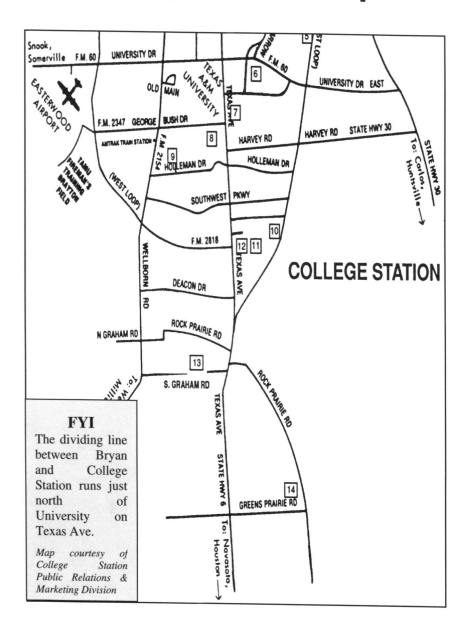

12

That's History

Bryan

In 1821, Steven Fuller Austin's colonists settled on choice lands along the Brazos and Colorado Rivers. Early settlements were established at Washington-on-the-Brazos, Independence and Hempstead.

Under the Imperial Colonization Law, families who settled in Austin's colony were required to farm the land, raise stock and become Roman Catholics and Mexican Citizens. The head of each family in compliance were given a league (4,428 acres) and a labor (177 acres) of land. Single men were would receive one third of that amount. Land was a strong incentive for U.S. citizens who could scarcely afford to purchase property back home.

Austin's nephew, William Joel Bryan, was among the first 300 families to settle the new Texas colony. Bryan acquired land in Brazos County and in 1861, he sold a single square-mile tract of land to the Houston and Texas Central Railroads. The $3,200 purchase would become a full-fledged city serving the railway, its' employees and passengers.

Officials of the two companies were so pleased with the transaction that they named the new town "Bryan" in honor of the colonist. In 1866, the Brazos County seat was moved from Boonville to Bryan.

Bryan became a bustling trade center with cotton, cattle and oil among its chief exports. This region of big plantations reached its' peak of agricultural prosperity following the Civil War.

In 1871, Bryan was incorporated and was selected by the State of Texas to be the site of the new Land Grant College. In 1876, the Agricultural and Mechanical College of Texas was established with an initial enrollment of forty students.

Bryan expanded its role as a regional educational center in 1886, when the Allen Academy and the Villa Maria Ursuline Academy for girls were established.

Although primarily an agricultural town, the 1900s saw a tremendous growth in Bryan's business and industry. By the late 1960s, the Brazos County Industrial Park was established to accommodate new enterprise. The Bryan Business Park followed fueling the development of new businesses.

Between 1960 and 1990, Bryan's population more than

> **FYI**
> When the City of Bryan was incorporated in 1871, President Ulysses S. Grant was in office.

The Texas A&M Corps of Cadets

number about 2,000 and produce more military officers than any other non-academy institution.

13

Photo: City of Bryan
Historic Downtown Bryan

doubled, creating an increasing demand for jobs, housing, products and services.

Today, Bryan has a vital and robust economy, quality schools, state-of-the-art healthcare, safe neighborhoods and a history that is reflected in the buildings and pride of her residents.

College Station

In 1831, the last of Steven F. Austin's colonists were moving into the Brazos Valley. Among the settlers was Richard Carter from Morgan County, Alabama.

Carter and his family were awarded one league of land (177 acres) on which to farm and raise livestock. Carter built a house on Saline Creek, which is known today as "Carter Creek." Much of Carter's 177 acres encompass what is today the City of College Station. The site was some two miles east of land that later became the Texas A&M University Campus.

The Morrill Land Grant Act of 1862, established a permanent fund from which agricultural and mechanical arts colleges could be started. The funding came from the sale of donated Federal lands.

In 1866, Texas accepted 180,000 acres for the endowment of a Land Grant Institution.

On April 17, 1871 the Agricultural and Mechanical College of Texas was officially, but not physically, established. Governor Edmund Davis appointed three commissioners, John G. Bell, F.E. Grothaus, and George B. Slaughter to select the site upon which to build the college.

14

Austin, Galveston, Waco and San Marcos were among a handful of towns which were considered as prospective sites for the new school. When it looked like Bellville was to be the commissioner's choice, Bryan resident, Harvey Mitchell spearheaded an effort to acquire and donate property for the campus. With the help of other residents, 2,416 acres of land were transferred to the A. and M. College. In the fall of 1871, construction began on Old Main, the college's first building.

During the initial 50 years, off-campus housing and commercial development grew slowly. Then in 1921, the Southside Development Company established College Park, a subdivision located south of campus. Other housing and commercial developments followed and in 1938, citizens voted 217 to 39 to incorporate the City of College Station.

Today, College Station is a vibrant, growth-oriented city with an increasingly diverse economy, excellent schools and subdivisions with amenities such as playgrounds, lakes and tennis courts.

Photo: City of Bryan (by Richard Gunn, 1957)
Autos and oil figure prominently in B-CS history

Photo: City of Bryan
Home on Bryan's Historic East Side

One More Night

Bryan-College Station is a magnet for visitors and newcomers. As such, local proprietors strive to accommodate the needs, preference and expectations of their guests. This chapter covers the bed and breakfasts, hotels/motels and recreational vehicle parks in the twin cities.

The accommodations presented here include a wide range of price and designs, ensuring that there is something for every taste and budget. If you see a place that isn't mentioned here, check it out – the options for overnight guests are expanding rapidly and we might not have found them all yet!

Prices vary depending upon the time of the week and availability. On special event weekends, expect to pay more for accommodations. Major credit cards are generally accepted, but it is wise to confirm which cards are honored when making reservations.

Handicapped-accessibility and specific needs should be addressed when making reservations. Pets are generally not allowed in Bed and Breakfasts or in hotels/motels. Also, smoking is usually permitted only in designated rooms. Finally, the facilities and amenities were designed to cater to individuals, couples, families and groups. So, if there is anything in particular that you need to make your stay more enjoyable, be sure to ask!

Photo: City of Bryan
Stay a while and see the sights!

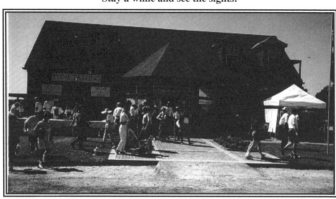

Photo: Rhonda Brinkmann
Nita Harding and Pam Dorsey operate Angelsgate and Dansby House B&Bs

Bed and Breakfasts

Several bed and breakfasts operate in Bryan-College Station offering a variety of amenities. The standard prices range from $50 per night to $150. As mentioned, expect to pay more on special event weekends.

Angelsgate
Four elegant suites are available in this 1909 Victorian-style B&B. Each room features a sitting area and a queen-sized bed. National Historical Landmark. 615 E. 29th St., (B) 779-1232.

Bonnie Gambrel
Three guestrooms, a honeymoon suite, pool and spa grace this circa 1913 home. National Registry of Historic Places. 600 E. 27th St. (B) 779-1022.

The Dansby Guest House
Built in 1902, the home is located on "Bankers Row" in Bryan. National Registry of Places. 611 E. 29th St. (B) 779-1997.

The Cottage at Twin Oaks
"A country setting only minutes from town." Two bedrooms in a contemporary home featuring the same great service as the Twin Oaks Bed and Breakfast which is operated by the same proprietor. 3909 F&B Rd. (CS) 260-9059.

The Flippen Place
Three comfortable guestrooms situated on 50 wooded acres. Originally, this 170 year-old home was an Amish Barn that was moved from Ohio. 1199 Haywood (CS) 693-7660.

Reveille Inn
A charming Colonial-style Inn decorated with Aggie Spirit in true A&M style. The home was once the Kappa Alpha fraternity house. 4400 Old College Road (B) 846-0858.

7F Land & Cattle Company Lodge
"Ralph Lauren meets Martha Stewart on Fantasy Island" describe these individual cabin suites situated on 20-acres. The decor of each cabin reflects one of the seven countries that flew a flag over Texas. 16611 Royder Road (Wellborn) 690-0073.

Twin Oaks Bed and Breakfast
Located near the University, this B&B once stood on the Texas A&M campus. 3905 F&B Road (B) 846-3694.

The Vintner's Loft at Messina Hof Wine Cellars
A secluded hide-a-way for two can be found at this country vineyard. Furnished with antiques, the room features a view of the pond and vineyard. 4545 Old Reliance Road (B) 778-9463.

Hotels and Motels

Hotel and motel rooms are plentiful and reasonably priced in Bryan-College Station. The following price codes are based upon the "rack-rate" quoted in a recent telephone survey. The rates reflect a one-night, mid-week stay for a single adult.

Hotel Price Codes
$ - Less than $35

$$- $36 to 50

$$$-$51 to $60

$$$$-$61 to $80

$$$$$-$81+

Prices are based on availability and may be increased on special event weekends such as Texas A&M home football or graduation weekends.

$$$ Best Western-Inn at Chimney Hill
96 guestrooms, airport shuttle, restaurant and outdoor pool. 901 University Drive East (CS) 260-9150.

$$ Brazos Inn
92 guestrooms, restaurant, and outdoor pool. 3113 Highway 21 East (B) 779-0020.

$ Casa Loma Motel
24 guestrooms. 2000 South Texas Avenue (B) 822-3728.

$ Cattleman's Inn
25 guestrooms and restaurant 1805 North Texas Ave. (B) 778-1971.

$$$$$ College Station Hilton
303 guestrooms, airport shuttle, restaurant and outdoor pool. 801 University Drive East (CS) 693-7500.

$$$ Comfort Inn
114 guestrooms, airport shuttle, outdoor pool. 104 Texas Ave. S. (CS) 846-7333.

$$ Days Inn
100 guestrooms, airport shuttle, restaurant and outdoor pool. 2514 Texas Ave. S. (CS) 696-6988.

$ El Camino Motel
14 guestrooms. 2102 Highway 21 East (B) 778-6262.

$ E-Z Travel Motor Inn
72 guestrooms. 2007 Texas Ave. S. (CS) 693-5822.

$$$$ Hampton Inn
135 guestrooms, airport shuttle, outdoor pool. 320 South Texas Ave. (CS) 846-0184.

$$$ Holiday Inn
126 guestrooms, airport shuttle, restaurant and outdoor pool. 1503 Texas Ave. S. (CS) 693-1736.

$ Holiday Plaza
33 guestrooms. 1720 South Texas Ave. (B) 822-3748.

$$$$ LaQuinta Motor Inn
176 guestrooms, airport shuttle, restaurant and outdoor pool. 607 Texas Ave. S. (CS) 696-7777.

$$$ Manor House Inn
115 guestrooms, airport shuttle, restaurant and outdoor pool. 2504 Texas Ave. S. (CS) 764-9540.

$$ MSC Guestrooms
41 guestrooms and restaurant. Memorial Student Center, TAMU (CS) 845-8909.

$$ Motel 6
110 guestrooms. 2327 Texas Ave. S. (CS) 696-3379.

$$ Preference Inn
115 guestrooms, restaurant and outdoor pool. 1601 Texas Ave. (B) 822-6196.

$$$$ Quality Suites
81 guestrooms, airport shuttle, outdoor pool. 1010 University Dr. E. (CS) 695-9500.

$$$ Ramada Inn
167 guestrooms, airport shuttle, restaurant and outdoor pool. 1502 Texas Ave. S. (CS) 693-9891.

$$ Relax Inn
60 guestrooms. 3604 Highway 21 East (B) 778-1881.

$ Texas Oaks Apartment Motel
21 guestrooms. 1800 S. Texas Ave. (B) 823-0612.

$ Varsity Inn
92 guestrooms, restaurant and outdoor pool. 3702 Texas Ave. S. (CS) 693-6810.

$$$$ Vineyard Court
48 guestrooms, outdoor pool. 1500 George Bush Drive East (CS) 693-1220.

Recreational Vehicle Parks

Recreational vehicle parks are popular in Bryan-College Station, especially during the cool spring and winter weather.

FYI
Pick up a *Discount Travel Guide* at a Tourist Information Center for money saving coupons on hotel stays.

Rates, including those with electric hook-ups, were less than $20 with most falling in the $10 range.

College Station RV Park
10 spaces, electric and water. 3905 F&B Road (CS) 846-3694.

Greenbriar Acres Mobile Home Park
15 spaces, electric and water. 1100 Turkey Creek Road (B) 823-8800.

Krenek's Mobile Home Park
31 spaces, shower, electric and water. 1602 Finfeather Road (B) 822-6697.

Oakwood Mobile Home Community
2 spaces, restrooms, electric and water. 920 Clearleaf Drive (B) 779-2123.

Primrose Lane Mobile Home & RV Park
109 spaces, outdoor pool, shower, electric and water. 2929 Stevens Drive (B) 778-0119.

Road-Runners Campground
24 spaces, electric and water. 3105 E. Villa Maria Road (B) 776-7314.

University RV Park
42 spaces, shower, electric and water. 19191 Highway 6 South (CS) 690-6056.

Village 21 RV Park
10 spaces, electric and water. 2405 Highway 21 East (B) 778-2733.

TAMU Elsie Duncan Olsen Grove Park
42 spaces, electric and water. George Bush Drive & Olsen Road (CS) 847-8694.

19

Craving Cuisine

In talking with restaurateurs one thing became quite clear – people in Bryan-College Station expect large portions of tasty cuisine at fair prices. Fortunately, many restaurants serve just that– generous helpings of delicious barbecue, steak, chicken, Mexican, Oriental and seafood dishes that fit almost any budget.

Some hometown eateries buy produce, herbs and meat from within the region, insuring freshness and contributing to a distinctly local taste. Many of these restaurants have reputations for delivering the best tastes in town.

Reservations are rarely needed and often not accepted except on Mother's Day, Easter, Thanksgiving or on other holidays. Expect a long wait or to be turned away from popular eateries on TAMU parents or home game weekends. We have tried to note where reservations are requested or in the rare instance, required.

We've grouped the restaurants by the type of food that is served rather than by location. In a community where almost everything is within a twenty-minute drive, the location of a restaurant seems secondary to taste.

The focus of this chapter is to highlight local, independent restaurants with fewer than three locations. We've tried to cover restaurants in all price ranges, which have earned a favorable local reputation. However, that doesn't mean that restaurants not included in this book should be avoided.

Hearty servings of familiar fare are dished up at chain restaurants located throughout the twin cities. For a quick meal, there are a variety of fast food restaurants to choose from. These eateries cluster along major by-ways such as Texas Avenue, Villa Maria, Briarcrest, University, Harvey and the Southwest Parkway.

Keep in mind that several hotels, quick marts and specialty shops serve a variety of prepared foods. Additionally, church suppers, roadside barbecues and street festivals offer alternative dining that is often delicious and easy on the pocketbook.

The dollar signs at the beginning of each entry indicate the average price for dinner for two without drinks, desert or a tip. The following key identifies the price range intervals:

Restaurant Price Codes	
$ - Less than $15	$$$- $25 to $40
$$-$15 to $25	$$$$- over $40

So, keep your eyes open as you travel the local roads and if a restaurant looks interesting – stop and feed your curiosity. With so many new eateries opening up, there's no telling what you'll find to suit your tastes!

Barbecue

$ Junior's Barbecue
With breakfast tacos and barbecue by the plate or by the pound, Junior's serves up good eating! Mon.-Sat. 6 a.m. – 8 p.m. 1660 San Jacinto (B) 823-2707.

$ Martin's Place
A third-generation family-owned barbecue eatery with beef, pork, ribs and sausage by the plate, pound or in sandwiches. Tues. – Fri. 10:30 a.m. – 8 p.m.; Sat. until 7 p.m. 3403 S. College Ave. (B) 822-2031.

$$ Tom's Bar-B-Que & Steakhouse
Locally renowned for The Aggie Special – beef, bread, pickle, onions and cheddar cheese served up on butcher paper.

Chicken fried steak, catfish and other favorites round out a hearty menu. Sun. – Thurs. 11 a.m. – 9 p.m.; Fri. – Sat. until 10 p.m. Two locations: 3610 S. College (B) 846-4275 and 2005 Texas Ave. S. (CS) 696-2076.

Burgers

$ Bullwinkles Grill & Bar
Fun food – burgers, fajitas and wings are on the menu at this local eatery. Twenty-six TV screens show sporting events and an interactive trivia game adds a little competition to every meal. Kitchen open Sun. – Thurs. 11 a.m. – 10 p.m. Fri. – Sat. until 11 p.m. Culpepper Plaza, 1601 S. Texas Ave. (CS) 696-9777.

Bryan-College Station

was named the fastest growing U.S. metropolitan area in terms of household growth.

Wall Street Journal, 1996

$ Burger Boy
Home of the "Hammer," a 1½ pound cheeseburger, fried mozzarella, shrimp dinner and other popular dishes. Mon.-Sat. 10:30 a.m. – 1 a.m.; Sun. 11 a.m. – 10:30 p.m. 311 Church St. (CS) 846-2146.

$ Chicken Oil Company
The "Death Burger," with jalapenos is the hottest burger in town. Check out the casual atmosphere, shoot a game of pool and enjoy a toasty fire on a cold night. Tues. – Sat. 11 a.m. – midnight; Sun. – Mon. 11 a.m. – 10 p.m. 3600 S. College Ave. (CS) 846-3306.

$ The Cow Hop
Enjoy the famous 1/3 pound hamburger with cheese, mushrooms and bacon, a Gardenburger or a chicken fried chicken. Daily, 11 a.m. - 10 p.m. 317 University Dr. (CS) 846-2496.

$ Koppe Bridge Bar and Grill
The "Best Big Burgers in Town," steak and chicken sandwiches round out a casual but tasty menu. Play pool, catch some live music on selected Saturday nights or watch your favorite sports team on the color TV. Mon. – Sat. 11:30 a.m. – 10 p.m. 12055 Wellborn Rd. (CS) 764-2933.

$ Margie's Bar & Grill
Old-fashioned burgers and hot dogs are served up along side chili, Frito pie and enchiladas. The food will bring you in but the pool tables and dominos will keep here for a while. Mon. – Thurs. 10 a.m. – 9 p.m.; Fri. – Sat until 10 p.m. 320 N. Main (B) 823-7032.

22

Deli

$ Farmer's Market Delicatessen
Hearty sandwiches, twice-baked potatoes, spaghetti and lasagna are among the offerings at this deli/restaurant. Fresh cakes, pastries and homemade breads are served daily. Mon. – Sat., 6 a.m. – 9 p.m. 2700 Texas Ave. (B) 823-6428.

$ Honey-B-Ham & Deli
A dazzling array of meats and cheeses are piled high on sourdough or other specialty breads. Fresh-made salads, pies and cookies highlight any meal. Mon. – Sat., 10 a.m. – 6 p.m. 2416 "A" Texas Ave. S. (CS) 696-DELI.

> **FYI**
> Oxford Street, Ninfa's and many other restaurants provide a free desert for anyone celebrating a birthday or anniversary.

Diners

$ Cattlemen's Inn Diner
Hand-battered chicken fried steak, onion rings, burgers and catfish are served up in a casual café atmosphere. Open 24 hours daily. 1805 N. Texas Ave. (B) 778-1971.

$ The Deluxe Diner
A 1950s style diner with burgers in baskets, cherry cokes, hand-breaded onion rings and Philly cheese fries. Start your day with a country-style breakfast complete with fresh squeezed orange juice, eggs any way you like them, home fries and a slab of ham. Sun. – Thurs. 7 a.m. – 10 p.m.; Fri. – Sat. until 11 p.m. 203 University Dr. (CS) 846-7466.

Fine Dining

$$ Café Eccell
This popular eatery has an almost indescribable menu with wood-fired pizzas, pasta and mesquite-grilled entrees and incredible deserts. Top off your meal with espresso or enjoy one of the many microbrews. Daily 11 a.m. – 10 p.m. 101 Church St. (CS) 846-7908.

$$ Clementine's Café
Skirted in the eclectic ambiance of the Old Bryan Marketplace, this gourmet restaurant and bakery dishes up elegant cuisine. Sautéed jumbo shrimp, seared pork tenderloin and Macadamia crusted mahi-mahi are just a few of this eatery's scrumptious entrees. Top off any meal with crème brulee, Cappuccino mousse or Bavarian cheesecake. 202 S. Bryan Ave. (located in the Old Bryan Marketplace) (B) 779-3245.

$ Kaffee Klatsch
The blackboard menu of home-cooked entrees changes daily at this elegant eatery. Chicken salad trio, spinach enchiladas, quiche, crepes and other tantalizing tastes await at this popular lunch and brunch spot. Reservations recommended. Tues. —Fri. 10 a.m. – 4 p.m.; Sat. 9 a.m. – 3 p.m.; Sun. 10 a.m. – 2 p.m. 108 North Ave. (B) 846-4360.

$$$$ Remedies
The area's most exclusive restaurant requires reservations – one to two weeks in advance is recommended. With steaks and seafood prepared for taste as well as show, this five-course experience provides a night to remember. Open for dinner on Wed., Fri. and Sat. 4660 Raymond Stolzer Pky.(CS) 260-1476.

$$$ Royers Café
The phrase "sophisticated comfort food" has been used to describe the unique but tantalizing menu at this highly

publicized café. Choose from pork tenderloins smothered in peach and pepper glaze, mahi-mahi, tender beef filets or other house specialties before succumbing to the temptation of homemade pie topped with Blue Bell ice cream. Sun., Tues., Wed., Thurs., 11 a.m. – 9:30 p.m.; Fri., 11 a.m. – 10:30 p.m.; Sat., 12 – 10:30 p.m. 2500 Texas Ave. S. (CS) 694-8826.

$$$$ The Texan

The oldest fine-dining establishment in Bryan offers an array of tempting tastes. Ethnic entrees from around the world are impeccably served along with such popular dishes as shrimp, prime rib and chicken. Live Boston lobsters are flown in daily. Reservations recommended. Wed. – Sat. 5-10 p.m. 3204 S. College (B) 822-3588.

$$$$ Vintage House at Messina Hof

Enjoy gourmet European cuisine right here in the Brazos Valley. A variety of wines are available to complement the meal. Reservations are recommended. Wed. – Sat. 11 a.m. – 2:30 p.m.; Sun., noon – 2:30 p.m.; Thurs. – Sat. 5 p.m. – 10 p.m. 4545 Old Reliance Road (B) 778-3138.

$$ Zum Schnitzel Haus

Old Town Bryan is the setting for German continental food. Seafood, steaks and fabulous deserts are prepared fresh daily. Wed. – Fri. 11:30 a.m. – 2 p.m.; Tues. – Sat., 6 p.m. – 10 p. m. 218 N. Bryan St. (B) 823-8974.

See "Night Clubs" p. 28

> **FYI**
> The Deluxe Diner was established in 1947 and in earlier years was called the "Handy Burger," "Onion Rings," and "Deluxe Burger Bar."

Hard-to-Describe, Hard-to-Resist

$$ Alicia's

A distinctly different flavor is served here – Tex-Mex-Cajun. Shrimp Creole enchiladas, crawfish fajitas and blackened chicken fajitas with refried beans and rice. Combination plates and specials available daily. Mon. – Thurs. 11 a.m. – 9 p.m.; Fri. – Sat. 11:30 a.m. – 10 p.m.; Sun. 11:30 a.m. – 4 p.m. 317 College Ave. (CS) 268-5333.

$$ The Grapevine

Shrimp Alfredo, Italian chicken rigatoni, and Santa Fe green enchiladas are featured at this popular establishment. Mon. – Sat. 10 a.m. – 9 p.m. 201 Live Oak (CS) 696-3411

$ Layne's of College Station

Home of the "Soon-to-be-famous chicken fingers," this place knows its' chicken! Daily 11 a.m. – 10 p.m. 106 Walton Dr. (CS) 696-7633.

$ Red Bandana

With barbecue, chicken fried steak and fajitas this popular eatery can satisfy any appetite. Mama Lois' famous pecan, apple, lemon chess and peach pies are proudly served here. Mon. – Thurs. 6 a.m. – 9 p.m.; Fri. – Sat. until 10 p.m.; Sun. 7 a.m. – 9 p.m. The East Bypass & Highway 21 (B) 778-0077.

$ Shannon's

Soul food is the order of the day on a menu that changes daily. Enjoy chicken and dressing, beef tips, black-eyed peas, cabbage or a peach cobbler to die for. Mon. – Sat. 6:30 a.m. – 6 p.m. 601 San Jacinto (B) 779-0842.

This 50s-style diner serves up delicious burgers, breakfasts and more!

$ Wenonah's Pantry
Fresh baked muffins, kolaches and scones are prepared at the café located in this gourmet kitchenware shop. Enjoy the "Chief's Special" which ranges from oriental chicken salad, to goulash. Complete any meal with an espresso or a wonderfully rich desert. Mon. – Fri. 7:30 a.m. – 7 p.m.; Sat., 8 a.m. – 6 p.m. 4301 S. Texas Ave. 846-8220.

$$ Wings N' More
Buffalo-style wings and tender baby-back ribs are the hallmarks of this popular restaurant. Soups, salads and a variety of meats top off a deliciously fun restaurant. 1045 S. Texas Ave. (CS) 693-6363 and 3230 Texas Ave S. (CS) 694-8966.

Hot Dogs

$ Dogs & Such
Breakfast burritos, chopped beef sandwiches, homemade chili and more varieties of hot dogs than you can shake a stick are this eatery's stock-in-trade. 701 University Drive E. (CS) 846-7877.

FYI

Many restaurants offer children's menus featuring burgers, chicken or other "kid friendly" cuisine. Entrees ordered off the kid's menu are usually less expensive than those off the standard menu.

$ Hot Dogs, Etc. Burgers & More
Three of the America's most favorite foods are staples at this hometown haunt - hot dogs, hamburgers and hot wings. End a fun meal with homemade cookies or brownies. Sun. – Thurs., 10:30 a.m. – midnight; Fri. – Sat., 10:30 a.m. – 2 a.m. 301 N. Texas Ave. (B) 822-3918.

Italian

$$$ Caffe' Capri
A local Italian eatery with an eclectic big city atmosphere serving fettuccini, cannelloni and other tasty dishes. Mon. – Thurs., 11 a.m. – 2 p.m. and 6 p.m. – 9 p.m.; Fri. – Sat., 5 p.m. – 9 p.m. 222 N. Main (B) 822-2675.

$ Mr. G's Pizzeria & Restaurant
Unbelievable calzone, fresh baked bread and delicious pizzas are the hallmark of this popular downtown spot. Mon. – Sat. 11 a.m. – 2 p.m. and 5 p.m. – 9 p.m. Closed Sun. 201 W. 26th St. (B) 822-6747.

Mexican

$$ Fajita Rita's
Beef and chicken fajitas, fresh tortillas and a variety of margaritas make every meal a fiesta! Sun. – Thurs., 11 a.m. – midnight. 4501 S. Texas Ave. (B) 846-3696.

$ Freebird's World Burrito Serving burritos chock full of fresh fillings such as beans, rice, tomatoes, lettuce and more. Sun. – Thurs., 11 a.m. – 10:30 p.m.; Fri. – Sat. to 11 p.m. 319 University Drive (CS) 846-9298 and 2050 Texas Ave. S. (CS) 695-0151.

$$ Garcia's Mexican Café
Authentic Mexican food at its best with quesadillas, enchiladas, chimichangas and more. Large portions, reasonable prices and wonderful margaritas. Sun. – Wed. 11 a.m. – 9:30 p.m.; Thurs., 11 a.m. – 10 p.m.; Fri – Sat. until 11 p.m. 1704 Kyle South (CS) 696-5900.

$ Gina's Restaurant Mexicano
Enchiladas, tacos and other tasty Mexican dishes are served up with a unique blend of northern and southern Mexican flavors. Tues. – Thurs. 11 a.m. – 9 p.m.; Fri. and Sat. until 10 p.m.; Sun. 8 a.m. – 9 p.m.; closed Mon. 300 N. Bryan (B) 822-1254.

$ Jose's
Delicious steak ranchero, carne Asada a la tamiqueno, fajitas and tacos al carbon are standard fare at this family owned and operated establishment. Tues. – Sun. 11 a.m. – 9:45 p.m. 3824 S. Texas Ave. (B) 268-0036.

See "Night Clubs" p. 28

FYI

Check out the local telephone directories for money saving coupons on meals.

$ Las Cascadas
Daily specials on traditional Mexican dishes including menudo and caldo de res are on the menu. Mon. – Fri. 10 a.m. – 11 p.m.; Sat. 8 a.m. – 11 p.m.; Sun. 8 a.m. – 8 p.m. 1601 S. Texas Ave. (B) 822-6260.

$ La Familia Taqueria
Serving fajitas, gorditas, caldo and more! Daily 6 a.m. – 9 p.m. 300 N. Texas Ave. (B) 822-9192 and 3702 Texas Ave. (CS) 695-0966.

$ Los Nortenos
Authentic Mexican flavors are stuffed into breakfast tacos, enchiladas and tacos al carbon. Sun. – Thurs. 7 a.m. – 10 p.m. Fri. – Sat. 7 a.m. – 11 p.m. 205 S. Main (B) 779-7337.

$ Saenz Tamales
Homemade tamales, chili, barbecue and fajitas are on the menu at this family owned restaurant. Daily 9 a.m. – 9 p.m. 1410 William Joel Bryan Pky. (B) 822-2700.

$$ Zarape's
Flautas, fajitas, chimichangas and popular Tex-Mex specialties are served up daily. Tues. – Sun., 10:30 a.m. – 9 p.m. 308 N. Main (B) 779-8702.

Oriental

$$ China Garden
Authentic and elegant describe this popular Chinese eatery. Enjoy General Tso; beef with broccoli or Flight of the Phoenix. Mon. – Fri., 11 a.m. – 2 p.m. and 5 p.m. – 9:30 p.m.; Sat. & Sun. 11 a.m. 2:30 p.m., Sat. night 5 p.m. – 10 p.m., Sun. night 5 p.m. – 9 p.m. 2901 S. Texas Ave. (B) 823-2818.

$ Chinese Food Restaurant
Belly up to the all-you-can eat buffet Mon. – Fri. and enjoy popular Chinese dishes. Mon. – Fri., 11 a.m. – 8 p.m.; Sat. 11 a.m. – 4 p.m. Closed on Sun. 1227 S. College Ave. (B) 779-0314.

$ Nipa Hot Restaurant
Serving a variety of Thai and Filipino dishes with meat, vegetables, rice and noodles. Mon. – Fri. 11 a.m. – 2:30 p.m., 5 p.m. – 9 p.m.; Sat. 11 a.m. – 2 p.m., 5 p.m. – 9 p.m.; Sun. 5:30 p.m. – 8:30 p.m. 405 University Drive W. 846-6090.

$ Sing Lee
A unique menu featuring Chinese, Japanese and Korean entrees. Enjoy egg rolls, steamed dumplings, fried bread and more. Daily 11 a.m. – 2 p.m. and 5 p.m. – 9:30 p.m. 3030 E. 29th St. (B) 776-4888.

Steaks

$$ La   Barronena   Ranch Steakhouse

Texas-size chicken fried steak, pork, seafood, spaghetti, and an assortment of thick, juicy steaks tempt the heartiest of appetites. Lunch: Mon. – Fri., 11 a.m.- 2 p.m.; Sat. – Sun., 11 a.m. – 3 p.m.: Dinner: Mon. –Thurs., 4:30 p.m. – 11 p.m.; Sat. 3 p.m. – 11 p.m.; and Sun., 3 p.m. – 9 p.m. 102 Live Oak (CS) 694-8232.

$$ Longhorn Tavern
Some of the best chicken fried steak in the county is served up at this popular spot. Chicken, catfish, frog legs, burgers and steaks round out a great menu. Mon. – Thurs., 11 a.m. – 9 p.m./ Fri. – Sat., 11 a.m. – 9:30 p.m.; closed Sun. 1900 Hwy. 21 E. (B) 778-3900.

$$$ T-Bone Jones
A Texas steakhouse known for its 18 ounce T-bone steak, alligator, and chicken fried steak. With a cigar room and pool tables, the casual atmosphere attracts native Texans and those who wish they were! Sun. – Thurs., 4 p.m. – 10 p.m.; Fri. – Sat., 4 p.m. – 11 p.m. 809 E. University (CS) 846-6823.

Photo: Rhonda Brinkmann
Many popular restaurants are located in Historic Downtown Bryan

Night Clubs

Trendy dancehalls and fancy theme clubs owned by the rich and famous aren't part of Bryan-College Station's nightlife. Instead, you'll find a friendly, warm atmosphere with cold drinks and hot music. Whether its dancing until dawn, shooting pool or talking into the wee hours, you're almost certain to find a favorite nightspot.

Alfred T. Hornbacks
Longnecks and pool. 4 p.m. – 1 a.m. daily. 120 Walton Dr. (CS) 693-4136.

Carney's Pub
One of the best beer selections in the Brazos Valley can be found at Carney's with some 50 brands of international and domestic brews. Stocked with pool tables shuffleboard, dartboards and a CD juke box. Mon. – Wed. 2 p.m. – 1 a.m., Thurs. – Fri. 4 p.m. – 1 a.m., Sat. and Sun. 5 p.m. – 1 a.m. 3410 S. College (B) 823-1294.

Club Ozone
Teen nights Mon. – Tues. 8 p.m. – midnight. Adults Tues. –Thurs. 8 p.m. – midnight, Fri. – Sat. 8 p.m. – 2 a.m. 103 Boyette (CS) 846-3195.

The Cowboy Club
Shoot pool, play darts or sing and dance to your favorite Country music. Mon. – Fri. 4 p.m. – 1 a.m., Sat. 7 p.m. – 1 a.m., closed Sun. 2820 Finfeather (B) 775-0494.

Crooked Path Ale House
Play darts, NTN Trivia and choose from an impressive array of beer on tap. Home of the Open Microphone Night for songwriters. Open 4 p.m. – 1 a.m. daily. 329 University Dr. (CS) 691-4624.

The Dixie Chicken
A 20+ year Aggie tradition with Longnecks, pitchers, burgers, dominos, pool tables and video games. Mon. – Sat. 10 a.m. – 1 a.m., Sun. noon – 1 a.m. 307 University Dr. (CS) 846-2322.

Dry Bean Saloon
Saloon and shot bar. Mon. – Thurs. 4 p.m. – 1 a.m., Fri. – Sat. 1 p.m. – 1 a.m., Sun. 6 p.m. – 1 a.m. 305 University Dr. (CS).

Duddley's Draw
Pool tables, video games, draft beer and Longnecks. Duddley's serves up sandwiches and soft tacos. Mon. – Sat. 11 a.m. – 1 a.m., Sun. noon – 1 a.m. 311 University Dr. (CS) 846-3030.

Fitzwilly's
A country bar and grill with burgers, hot wings and nachos. Play darts, dominoes, pool, shuffleboard and foosball. Live music on Thurs. and Saturdays. Daily 11 a.m. – 1 a.m. 303 University Dr. (CS) 846-8806.

> **FYI**
> Many night clubs provide free coffee, iced tea or soft drinks to designated drivers.

28

Hurricane Harry's
Pool tables and Longnecks. Thurs. –
Sun. 8 p.m. – 2 a.m. 313
College Ave. (CS) 846-
1724.

Ptarmigan Club
The oldest bar in Bryan
offers dancing,
Longnecks and hors d'
oeuvres. Mon. – Thurs.
7 p.m. – 10 p.m., Fri. 3
p.m. – 1 a.m., Sat. 6
p.m. – 1 a.m. 2005 S.
College (B) 822-2263.

FYI
Songwriters perform
original music weekly at
Open Microphone
Night. Sponsored by
Crooked Path Ale
House and KORA. Call
776-KORA for
information.

Shadow Canyon
A classic Texas Dance Hall with
dance lessons offered during spring
and fall semesters. Tues. – Sat. 6
p.m. – 1 a.m. 217 University Dr.
(CS) 846-4440.

The Tap
Watch sports on 20 TVs, Play NTN
Trivia, and rock to the sound of the
jukebox. Free peanuts issued at the

door – pitch the shells on the floor.
Daily 7 p.m. – 1 a.m. except closed on
Sun. 815 Harvey Rd.
(CS) 696-5570.

Texas Hall of Fame
Live music every Sat.
night and scheduled
concerts. Longnecks
and a real Texas Dance
Hall atmosphere. Tues.
– Sat. 8 p.m. – 1 a.m.
2305 FM 2818 (CS)
822-2222.

Yesterdays
Pool tables,
shuffleboard, darts
and video games.
Sun. – Thurs. noon
– 1 a.m., Fri. – Sat.
noon – 2 a.m., 4421
S. Texas Ave. (B)
846-2625.

Photo: Rhonda Brinkmann
University Drive in College Station is home to a number of popular night spots

Must Shop!

Some shoppers measure the quality of life by how many antique or used bookstores they visit. Others seemingly spend a lifetime at gigantic malls or searching for the most unique clothing or specialty shops. Fortunately, Bryan-College Station has something to offer even the most discriminating shoppers.

Everything from resale shops to fine jewelry stores dot Bryan-College Station's retail landscape. For a casual, climate controlled shopping excursion, visit area malls, strip centers and department stores. The road warriors of the consuming world can shift into over-drive and tour the area's many independent specialty stores. We have pulled together a list of some of our favorite "must shop" retailers. But, the list is by no means exhaustive. New shops are opening all the time so there's no telling what you might find - if you just look.

Often, specialty stores cluster together on the same street, so after visiting a retailer, ask what other "must shop" stores are nearby. Drive around and enjoy the experience of discovering new shops on your own.

As we mentioned in our "Getting Around" chapter, Bryan-College Station's by-ways are visitor-friendly. Take a look at the map, have a payment plan in mind and shop-till-you-drop!

Shopping Centers

Post Oak Mall

Six department stores, over 100 specialty shops, a three-screen movie theater and more than a dozen restaurants make shopping a real pleasure. Located at 1500 Harvey Road, (CS) Open M-S, 10AM-9PM, Sun., noon – 6PM. 764-0060.

Manor East Mall

Home to Bealls, Montgomery Wards and several specialty stores, the mall has been a shopping tradition for the working family for over 20 years. The mall is currently being updated and new tenants such as Family Dollar are being added to accommodate the value conscious shopper. Located at the corner of Villa Maria and Texas Ave. (B) Open daily. Individual store hours vary.

Antiques Stores

Antique stores are a lot like people – I've never met one that I didn't like and no two are exactly the same! The hours and type of merchandise vary from store to store, so it is a good idea to telephone ahead to verify business hours and what type of merchandise is in stock.

Amity Antiques
300 W. 26th (B) 822-7717.

Antique Shop, The
612 S. Hutchins (B) 775-4519.

Attic, The
118 S. Bryan (B) 822-7830.

Brazos Trader Antiques
210 W. 26th (B) 775-2984.

Bry-Mac Antiques
202 W. 26th (B) 775-7875.

Cavitt Corner Used Books & Collectibles
2100 Cavitt Ave (B) 822-6633.

Circa Antiques
201 N. Main (B) 823-4153.

Clocks & Collectibles
900 Harvey Rd. (CS) 693-7004.

Corner of Time Antique Mall
118 N. Bryan Ave. (B) 822-7400.

Gazebo Antiques
3828 S. College Ave. (B) 846-0249.

Main Street Antiques
113 N. Main (B) 822-6536.

Migration Antiques
419 N. Main (B) 822-9007.

Old Bryan Market Place
202 S. Bryan Ave. (B) 779-3245.

Tin Barn Antiques & Collectibles
3218 S. Texas Ave. (B) 779-6573.

Vintage Furnishings – Home & Office
1501 Fm Rd 2818 (CS) 693-0396.

Book - Used

BCS Books & Comics
A "must shop" for the casual comic reader or for the serious collector. The store also caries paperback fiction. 701 Inwood Dr. (B) 846-7412.

Carousel Paperbacks
New and used books tantalize the bibliographic taste buds at this shop. Carousel serves up best sellers, classics, mystery, science fiction, romance, children's and general interest paperback titles. Child play area and great "trade in" program. 1120 Harvey Rd. (CS) 696-7307.

Cavitt Corner Used Books & Collectibles
For an eclectic assortment of unique bibliographic treasures, check out this shop. Browse the stacks of paperback and hardcover volumes covering most genres. 2100 Cavitt Ave. (B) 822-6633.

Half Price Books Records Magazines
Filled with a huge selection of paperback and hardcover titles across all subjects for half-price or less. Offering new, used and rare editions. 3828 S. Texas Ave. (B) 846-2738.

Joe's Books
A classic second-hand bookstore with stack after stack of used, rare and unique volumes. Comfortable chairs add to the homey atmosphere enticing browsers to sit and read a spell. 1710 George Bush Dr. (CS) 693-4499.

Children's

Jacque's Toys & Books
Carries high quality, hard-to-find but easy-to-play with toys and books. Offers a variety of child-centered activities including story time and theme-birthday parties. 4301-A South Texas Ave. (B) 846-8660.

Once Upon a Child
This bright, well-appointed shop has new and gently used children's clothing, toys, equipment and books. The shop buys and sells used kid stuff in good condition. 2220 Texas Ave. S. (CS) 696-7161.

Fishing

The Bait Barn
The best in live bait and tackle for the recreational or serious fisherman. A variety of minnows, worms, perch, crawfish and more! 2704 E Hwy 2 (B) 778-3056.

Garden and Produce

Producer's Cooperative Assoc.
Green thumbs and the horticulturally challenged will find a wide selection of garden and lawn equipment and supplies. Children love feeding the koi fish in the pond out front and petting the store cat. 1800 N. Texas Ave. (B) 778-6000.

Steep Hollow Gardens
Nearly hidden from view on FM 1179 sits the home and business of Carol Patterson May. Only a small sign and the strikingly lush plants and gardens assure visitors that they have found the fabled Steep Hollow Gardens. Towering oaks shade shoppers as they browse through the Hummingbird, Culinary, Edible Flower and other specialty gardens. Steep Hollow Gardens offers an assortment of botanicals including herbs, flowering plants, and a variety of native Texas plants, many of which are on display. 7361 FM 1179 (B) 776-5452.

Farmer's Market
Homegrown squash, tomatoes, potatoes, peppers and other delectable fruits and vegetables are the order of the day at Bryan's Farmer's Market. The market is open on Saturday mornings beginning at 6:30 AM from about mid-May until mid-October. Local growers gather at the corner of Bryan and William J. Bryan Park Way in the Perry's parking lot with trucks loaded with fresh produce.

Gourmet

Wenonah's Pantry
Pamper the chef in your household with top-of-the-line kitchen gadgets, elegant tableware and a tasty assortment of specialty foods. An in-store café offers a variety of teas, coffees, and entrees. 4301 South Texas Ave. (B) 846-8220.

Pottery and Crafts

Joy Pottery
Functional, yet beautiful stoneware is the specialty of potter Rachel Norris. The hand-thrown pottery is dishwasher, oven and microwave safe. Norris takes custom orders and offers demonstrations and classes in pottery. In a drop-dead gorgeous setting next to a large pond, Joy Pottery is a great outing for the entire family. 4544 Old Reliance Road (B) (Across from Messina Hof. 778-1323.

Craftmasters' Mall
Touted as a "year-round arts and crafts show," this is a mandatory stop for all craft lovers. A huge selection of handcrafted specialty items is on display including Aggie, Texas,

seasonable and other one-of-a-kind crafts are offered at over 180 booths. 1857 Briarcrest Drive (B) 776-0870.

Hats

Catalena Hatters

To the uninitiated, a hat is just a hat. But to the cowboy, hats are a highly individualized item. Even if you don't know the difference between an Old-time Cowboy, Buckaroo, or Dude hat, the fine folks at Catalena can fix you up. Visit the store in downtown Bryan to pick up a new hat or to have one cleaned or renovated. 203 N. Main (B) 822-4423.

FYI
Look in local newspapers and in your mail box to find money saving coupons and sale announcements for local shops.

Sporting Goods

Play it Again Sports

As a supplier of new and used sports and fitness equipment, Play it Again Sports is a "must shop" stop for the recreational and serious sports enthusiast. The shop specializes in golf and exercise equipment but also offers a great assortment of bats, sticks, balls, skates, cleats and other gear. This is a popular store for parents in search of soccer, baseball, and other sports shoes and equipment for their little athletes. 2218 Texas Ave. S. (CS) 764-8285.

Texas

The Texas Store

Take home the flavor and flair of the Lone Star State with something from this unique shop. Hot sauces, chips, chili, candies, cookbooks, Western art, T-shirts, and other gift items await

both Texans and those who wish they were! 1500 Harvey Road (CS) 693-2061.

Unique and Unusual

Old Bryan Market Place

For 35 years this warehouse-style building was home to a hardware store. Today, it's over 20,000 square feet are chock full of antiques, furniture and specialty gift items. The shop is a surprisingly eclectic mix of old and new. Organized it's not, but the disarray adds to the shopper's sense of discovery and enjoyment. 202 S. Bryan Ave. (B) 779-3245.

The Garden District

Tucked away in a residential area in South Bryan, lies a shopping experience designed to awaken the

senses. The mellow sounds of wind chimes blowing in the breeze, lush greenery and a cool pond greet visitors to The Garden District. A handful of unique shops fill the neo-antebellum home that is the centerpiece of the district. Dried floral arrangements, live plants, children's clothing, jewelry and other specialty gifts are plentiful. Pamper yourself at the salon after enjoying a leisurely lunch at the café. 106-108 North Avenue (B) 846-1448.

See the Sights

Residents may sometimes take it for granted but there is certainly a lot to do right here in Bryan-College Station. Where else can you harvest and stomp grapes, stroll through the life of a President of the United States or paint a Volkswagen? The Messina Hof Winery, George Bush Presidential Library and Museum and The Children's Museum offer all of this and more! We haven't even scratched the surface of the many local attractions that make Bryan-College Station a most enjoyable and interesting place to visit or live.

Keep in mind that hours of operation and admission fees may change so it is wise to call ahead to confirm the information provided below.

Many other attractions are included in the Arts and Culture, Park It! and Must Shop! chapters so be sure and check them out as well.

So, take an hour, a day, a weekend or longer to explore some of the most accessible "big city-type" attractions right here in our own hometown!

Adamson Lagoon

Make a splash this summer at Bryan-College Station's own "mini Water Park." Adamson Lagoon is fun for the whole family! A large water slide, stump slide, tadpole slide, lily pads, water basketball, diving board and rental tubes make staying cool a real blast. Be sure and bring a Coast Guard approved life jacket for small tots – no water wings allowed. Open May-August, Mon.-Thurs. 1 p.m. –7:30 p.m.; Fri. 2 p.m. –7:30 p.m.; Sat. – Sun. noon –7 p.m. Admission $3.50. 1900 Anderson at Bee Creek Park. (CS) 764-3735.

Brazos Valley Museum of Natural History

Discover the wonders of nature at this cornucopia of science. View fossils, rocks and live animals including an opossum, a tarantula and several species of turtles and snakes. Let the kids learn about the local environs at the museum's Summer Nature Camp. Permanent and traveling exhibits give visitors something fun to think about!

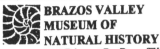

BRAZOS VALLEY MUSEUM OF NATURAL HISTORY
3232 Briarcrest Dr., Bryan, TX
(409) 776-2195

Summer Nature Camps
Second week of June through first week of August

Permanent Exhibit of Ice Age Mammals of the Brazos Valley

Traveling Exhibits throughout the year
(Exhibits planned for 1998-99: ARTIFACTS
FROM LA SALLE'S LA BELLE, BEASTS AND
HUNTERS OF THE ICE AGE, SEREGENTI
REFLECTIONS and THE TEXAS COWBOYS)

Science Exhibits / Family Programs

Birthday Parties / Nature Trail

Discovery Room with Live Animals

Museum Store

Up-coming exhibits include "From the Good Earth: A Celebration of Growing Food Around the World (Oct. 21, 1998 – Jan. 19, 1999), "Artifacts from de La Salle's La Belle" (Nov. 1, 1998-Dec. 31, 1998) and "The Texas Cowboys" (Sept. 1999-Oct. 1999). 3232 Briarcrest Drive (in the Brazos Center) (B) 776-2195 Open Tues. – Sat. 10 a.m. – 5 p.m. Closed Dec. 24-28 and Jan. 1st. Admission $6 adults; $5 members, senior citizens and students; $4 each for a group of ten that books in advance; children five years and younger admitted free. 3232 Briarcrest Dr. (B) 776-2195.

◆◆◆◆◆◆◆

Brazos County

is the third fastest growing county in the U.S. in terms of population growth.
American Demographics, 1996

Brazos Valley Telephone Museum

Do you know what a Swedish-American fiddle-back magneto wall telephone looks like? Well at the telephone museum you can get a look at this Victorian beauty. The Aggieland Telephone Pioneer Club sponsors the museum to help visitors learn about the history of telephony. The collection, which consists of about 300 items covers telephone history when the phones had more character than today's high-tech cell phones. Open Sun. 2 p.m. – 5 p.m.; group tours by appointment. Donations accepted. 422 Dellwood (B) 779-3414.

Bryan Historic Homes and Buildings

If you love architecture, history or just getting out in the sunshine you'll want to visit Historic Bryan. A traditional central business district reminiscent of an early Western town with a sprinkling of Victorian-style homes await you. Sprawling east and west of Texas Avenue near to, and including Downtown Bryan. See the list of National Register Properties on page 38.

Photo: City of Bryan
Harvest time at Messina Hof

Photo: Rhonda Brinkmann
George Bush, Jimmy Carter, Gerald Ford and Bill Clinton were among the many distinguished guests at the 1997 opening of the George Bush Presidential Library and Museum

The Children's Museum of the Brazos Valley

The Children's Museum is a kid-friendly collection of fun things to do and see. Children of all ages can paint a Volkswagen, shop for groceries, become actors on a stage and more. Learning through play can foster a life-long passion for learning. Open Wed. – Sat. 10 a.m. – 5 p.m., Sun 1 p.m. –5 p.m. Admission $3 per person, Senior's $2.75, Children under 1 year-old admitted free. Various memberships available. 202 S. Bryan St. (Next to Old Bryan Marketplace). (B) 779-KIDS.

Photo: Rhonda Brinkmann
Paint a VW at the Children's Museum

♦ ♦ ♦ ♦ ♦ ♦ ♦
Bryan-College Station
was named the fourth smartest city in the U.S. with 17.2% of the residents having at least a four-year college degree.
Fortune, 1997

♦ ♦ ♦ ♦ ♦ ♦ ♦
Texas A&M
is one of the top ten schools based on alumni financial support.

Bryan National Historic Buildings

Carnegie Library, 101 S. Main (circa 1903)
Cavitt House, 713 E. 30th St. (circa 1878)
Temple Freda, 205 Parker St. (circa 1913)
Kemp House, 606 W. 17th St. (circa 1922)
Moore House, 500 E. 25th St. (circa 1880)
Travis Elementary School, 901 E. 25th St. (circa 1927)
First State Bank & Trust, 100 W. 25th St. (circa 1930)
Astin Building, 106 W. 26th St. (circa 1917)
James Building, 200 W. 26th St. (circa 1906)
St. Andrew's Episcopal Church, 217 W. 26th St. (circa 1914)
Astin House, 508 W. 26th St. (circa 1921)
Oliver House, 602 W. 26th St. (circa 1904)
Municipal Building, 100 blk, E. 27th St.
McDougal-Jones House, 600 E. 27th St.(circa 1917)
Home at 604 E. 27th (circa 1920s)
Jenkins House, 607 E. 27th St. (circa 1892)
English Dansby House, 204 W. 28th St.
English-Poindexter House, 206 W. 28th St.
Blazek House, 409 W. 30th St. (circa 1920)
Wulkerson Home, 603 E. 31st St. (circa 1926)
Stone House, 715 E. 31st St. (circa 1925)
Home at 314 Baker St.
Humpty Dumpty Store, 218 N. Bryan St. (circa 1925)
Bryan Compress & Warehouse, 911 N. Bryan St.
Smith-Barron House, 100 S. Congress (circa 1912)
Parker House, 200 S. Congress (circa 1885)
Edge House, 609 S. Ennis (circa 1920)
Jones House, 812 S. Ennis (circa 1930)
C.S.P.S. Lodge, 304 N. Logan
First National Bank & Trust, 120 N. Main (circa 1919)
Allen Building, 400 N. Main (entire block circa 1890-1920)
Parker Lumber Company, 419 N. Main (circa 1910)
Masonic Temple, 107 S. Main (circa 1910)
Howell Building, 200 W. Main (circa 1906)
Bryan Ice House, 100 W. MLK (circa 1912)
Shotgun House, 407 N. Parker
Moto House, 900 N. Parker
Chance House, 102 S. Parker
St. Anthony's Catholic Church, 306 S. Parker (circa 1896)
Home at 109 N. Sterling (circa 1905)
Higgs House, 609 N. Tabor
Allen Academy Memorial Hall, 1100 Blk. Ursuline (circa 1914)
Allen House, 1120 Ursuline (circa 1915)
Armstrong House, 1200 Ursuline (circa 1910)
Zimmerman House, 308 W. Washington
Home at 600 W. Washington
Sausley House, 700 W. Washington

George Bush Presidential Library and Museum

Visit the tenth presidential library administered by the National Archives, to experience the life and presidency of George Bush. Artifacts, documents, film, interactive video, music and photographs provide a rare glimpse into Bush's distinguished public career as Congressman, Chief of the U.S. Liaison Office in China, Chairman of the Republican National Committee, Director of the Central Intelligence Agency, Vice-President and President.

History comes alive with the museum's larger exhibits including a World War II Avenger Torpedo Bomber, a 1947 Studebaker, a piece of the Berlin Wall and replicas of Bush's Camp David and Air Force One offices.

Open Mon. – Sat. 9:30 a.m. – 5:00 p.m.; Sun. noon – 5:00 p.m.; closed Thanksgiving, Christmas and New Year's Day. Admission: Adults $3, Kids 16 and under free, Senior Citizens, students, A&M and Blinn Faculty, and groups $2.50. 1000 George Bush Drive West (on Texas A&M's West Campus) (CS) 260-9552.

Messina Hof Winery

A unique blending of winemaking traditions from Messina, Italy and Hof, Germany has produced the most award-winning wines in Texas. Tour the vineyard, named the best East Texas attraction by the East Texas Tourism Association, dine at the Vintage House Sicilian Tratoria or escape the chaos of everyday living at the secluded Vintner's Loft Bed & Breakfast. Tours Mon. – Fri. 1 p.m., 2:30 p.m.; Sat. 11 a.m., 12:30 p.m., 2:30 p.m., 4 p.m.; Sun. 12:30 p.m., 2:30 p.m. Tour admission $3. (Editors Note: See the "Must Shop" chapter for details on Joy Pottery, which is located across the street from the vineyard. 4545 Old Reliance Road (B) 778-9463.

Texas A&M

To visitors and residents of Bryan-College Station, Texas A&M is more than just a world-class university. It is a passport to many exciting area attractions and a ticket to scores of music, sporting, and other special events. Included here are a few campus sites to see, but do yourself a favor – take a tour. Call MSC Hospitality at 845-1515 during the week or contact the information center at J. Earl Rudder Center at 845-5851 Mon. – Fri. 8 a.m. – 5 p.m. and Sat. 9 a.m. – 1 p.m. to schedule a campus tour. The J. Earl Rudder Center tour is geared more toward prospective students and their families but can also serve as a great introduction into the history and traditions of Texas A&M. There are so many interesting things to see on campus – why not try to see them all?

Check out the **Floral Test Gardens**, which produce between 800 and 1,000 different varieties of seeds and bulbs each year. The gardens are located on Houston St. near the Clayton W. Willams Jr. Alumni Center.

The Benz Gallery of Floral Art named for the late M. "Buddy Benz, a floral designer and teacher houses paintings, sculptures, ceramics, gold orchids and other exhibits. In the Horticultural and Forest Science Center on Horticultural Blvd. On West Campus.

The J. Wayne Stark University Center Gallery and the **Forsyth Gallery** are open Tues. – Fri. 9 a.m. – 8 p.m.; Sat. – Sun. noon – 6 p.m. Both galleries feature a variety of exhibits. Located in the Memorial Student Center on Joe Routt Blvd.

Listen on the hour and on the half to hear the chimes of the campus' **Albritton Bell Tower**. A total of 49 bells cast in France, weighing 17 tons ring from the tower at Old Main Drive just off Wellborn Rd.

See the beautiful **Centennial Wood Carvings** in the Memorial Student Center located on Joe Routt Blvd.

Travel back to the days of the Old West, visit the **Historic Texas Cattle Brands Collection** at the Kleberg Animal and Food Science Center on Agronomy Road (West Campus).

Few people think of Texas A&M without seeing an image of a Corps Cadet in their minds-eye. To learn more about the Corps of Cadets, visit **The Sam Houston Sanders Corps of Cadets Visitors Center**. The Sanders and Metzger Gun Collection with over 600 firearms, as well as 600 photographs, 79 Aggie rings and over 1000 artifacts are on display daily. Open Mon. – Fri. 8 a.m. – 5 p.m. and on some special event weekends. On campus between Throckmorton and Coke Streets 862-2862.

Depending upon the time of year, consider taking in a football, basketball, baseball or other sporting event at Texas A&M. Call the A&M ticket office at 845-2311 for information.

Once a Year

When something works... Bryan-College Station sticks with it. That's why the twin cities have so many wonderful annual events to look forward to. Each event is packed full of fun and tradition so make a point to be in town to enjoy them all.

Given that the actual dates vary from year to year, the events are listed in the months in which they normally are held. When possible, the previous location and a contact organization has been provided for each event. We recommend that you call for information the month prior to the scheduled event.

January

Martin Luther King Celebration
The Lincoln Center (CS) College Station Parks Dept. 764-3773.

Go Texan Days
Brazos County Pavilion (B).

Trout Fish-Out
Adamson Lagoon (CS) College Station Parks Dept. 764-3773.

Brazos Valley Boat and Sport Show
Brazos Center (B) 776-8338.

Faster than Molasses 10K/5K Fun Run, 1 Mile Walk
Southwood Athletic Park, (CS) College Station Parks Dept. 764-3773.

Kid Fish
Central Park (CS) College Station Parks Dept. 764-3773.

OPAS Gala
Hilton Hotel (CS) OPAS 845-1661.

February

Antique Show
(B) Brazos Center 776-8338.

Sweetheart Weekend
(B) Messina Hof Winery 778-9463.

New Car Dealers Automobile Show
(B) Brazos Center 776-8338.

Mardi Gras Brazos Style
Palace Theater (B) Bryan Main Street 821-3409.

Marriage of the Port
(B) Messina Hof Winery 778-9463.

March

Easter at the Creek
Held on Easter Morning (either in March or April). Wolf Pen Creek Amphitheater (CS) College Station Parks Dept. 764-3486.

Homebuilders Home & Garden Show
(B) Brazos Center 776-8338.

Winemaker's Birthday Party
(B) Messina Hof Winery 778-9463.

Brazos County Youth Livestock Show
Brazos County Pavilion (B).

Straight Shot 10K, 5K Run, 5K Fitness Walk
(CS) College Station Parks Dept. 764-3773.

FYI

The Bryan-College Station Convention and Visitor Bureau has the inside scoop on annual events. Give them a call at 260-9898.

Photo: City of Bryan
Annual Events are plentiful in B-CS

Police Department's Easter Egg Hunt
Central Park, (CS) College Station Parks Dept. 764-3773.

April
Easter at the Creek
Held on Easter Morning (either in March or April). Wolf Pen Creek Amphitheater (CS) College Station Parks Dept. 764-3486.

Noon Tunes Concerts
Every Thurs. at noon. Palace Theater (B) Bryan Main Street 821-3409.

Chamber of Commerce Trade Show
Brazos Center (B), Chamber of Commerce 260-5200.

March of Dimes WalkAmerica
(B-CS).

Run Through the Vines
(B) Messina Hof Winery 778-9463.

Wine and Roses Festival
(B) Messina Hof Winery 778-9463.

Home and Garden Tour & Luncheon
(B) The Women's Club 822-5019.

Grunt and Grind Biathlon
(CS) College Station Parks Dept. 764-3773.

Kinder Fest
(B) Bryan Parks 361-3658.

Arbor Day Celebration
(CS) College Station Parks Dept. 763-3773.

Arbor Day Celebration
Bryan Regional Athletic Complex (B) Bryan Parks Dept. 361-3656.

May
Noon Tunes Concerts
Every Thurs. at noon. Palace Theater (B) Bryan Main Street 821-3409.

Cinco De Mayo Celebration
The Lincoln Center (CS) College Station Parks Dept. 764-3773.

"Can Run" 5K Run and 1 Mile Walk
(CS) College Station Parks Dept 764-3773.

Cinco De Mayo Concert
Wolf Pen Creek Amphitheater (CS) College Station Parks Dept. 764-3773.

End of Semester Bash
Wolf Pen Creek Amphitheater (CS) College Station Parks Dept. 764-3486.

Jazz and Blues Festival
Wolf Pen Creek Amphitheater (CS) College Station Parks Dept. 764-3486.

Spring Art Market
(CS) Post Oak Mall 764-0060.

June
Bryan Bluegrass Festival
Lake Bryan (B) Bryan Parks Dept. 361-3658.

Fishing Derby
Cy Miller Pond (CS) College Station Parks Dept. 764-3773.

Juneteenth Celebration
The Lincoln Center (CS) College Station Parks Dept. 764-3773.

Port & Cream Weekend
(B) Messina Hof Winery 778-9463.

Texas Music Festival
TAMU Music Program (CS) 845-3355.

July

July 4th Celebration
Olsen Field (CS).

Brazos Heritage Society July 4th Celebration
Heritage Park (B) Brazos Heritage Society Julie Schultz 774-4079.

Merchants & Business Association July 4th Celebration
Downtown Bryan (B) Bryan Main Street 775-7875.

Paddle Wheel Biathlon
Southwood Athletic Park (CS) College Station Parks Dept. 764-3773.

Antique Show
(B) Brazos Center 776-8338.

Pickers Club Harvest Weekend
(B) Messina Hof Winery 778-9463.

Harvest Evening Concerts
(B) Messina Hof Winery 778-9463.

Back to School Fashion Show
College Station Conference Center (CS) 764-3720.

FYI
Christmas in the Park is great fun for the whole family! Enjoy a dazzling display of holiday lights, sing along with your favorite carols or take a ride in a horse drawn buggy. Call College Station Parks Dept. at 764-3773 for schedule information.

August

Pickers Club & Harvest Weekend
(B) Messina Hof Winery 778-9463.

Bluebonnet Street Rodders Club
Central Park (CS) College Station Parks Dept. 764-3773.

September

Diez Y Seis Celebration
Downtown Bryan (B) Bryan Main Street 821-3409.

Chamber of Commerce Golf Tournament
B-CS Chamber of Commerce 260-5200.

October

Antique Show
(B) Brazos Center 776-8338.

Historic Homes Tour
(B) Brazos Heritage Society Julie Schultz 774-4079.

Octoberfest
(B) Bryan Parks Dept. 361-3658.

November

OPAS Fashion Show & Luncheon
(CS) OPAS 845-1661.

Wine Premier
(B) Messina Hof Winery 778-9463.

Texas Country Christmas Tours
(B) Messina Hof Winery 778-9463.

December

Texas Country Christmas Tours
(B) Messina Hof Winery 778-9463.

Bryan Lighting Ceremony
Bryan Municipal Building (B) Bryan Parks Dept. 361-3656.

Photo: City of Bryan
Some of the best things in Bryan-College Station only come around once a year!

Arts and Crafts Show
(B) Brazos Center 776-8338.

Christmas in the Park Lighting Ceremony and Open House
Central Park (CS) College Station Parks Dept. 764-3773.

Jingle Bell Run
Texas Ave. Holiday Parade Route (CS) College Station Parks Dept. 764-3773.

Holiday Parade
Texas Ave. at New Main to Texas Ave. at Sulphur Springs (B) Downtown Main Street 775-7875.

Holiday High Tea
Brazos Heritage Society (B) Julie Schultz 774-4079.

Parade of Lights Tour
(B) Bryan Parks Dept. 361-3656.

Bryan-College Station

is the fifth fastest growing city in the U.S. in terms of population growth.

Kiplinger's Personal Finance, **1997**

Arts and Culture

Bryan-College Station is exhibiting growth in many areas due to the mushrooming population and tourist trade. An increasing number of arts-related activities and cultural programs is further evidence of this trend.

The Arts Council of the Brazos Valley is the umbrella organization that coordinates much of the arts and cultural activities in Bryan-College Station. For over 25 years, the council has promoted and supported the arts through special events, grants, scholarships, awards and a local gallery.

If you have any questions about the arts in Bryan-College Station, call the Arts Council of the Brazos Valley at 696-ARTS.

Both the visual and performing arts are included in this chapter, so by all means, enjoy the arts in Bryan-College Station!

Photo: City of Bryan
The arts are something to sing about!

TIMOTHY W. VANYA

is showing at

THE RED BRICK STUDIOS & GALLERY

Features the Aggie "Maroon Collection" of Fine Art
and the "Final Review" Boot and Saber Cases

202 S. Bryan, Historic Downtown Bryan, Texas, 77803
(409) 775 - 3796   1(800) 460 - 3321

Call for Gallery Hours   Ten Minutes from Campus

Art Galleries

Benz Gallery of Floral Art
A collection of paintings, sculptures, ceramics and more. Located in the Horticultural and Forest Sciences Building on Texas A&M's West Campus. 845-1699 Mon. – Fri. 8 a.m. – 5 p.m.

Forsythe
Home of Bill and Irma Runyon's art collection. Includes a sparkling display of American cut glass and English cameo glass. Especially enjoyable are the paintings by American & French Impressionists. Located on the main floor in the Memorial Student Center on the Texas A&M Campus. 845-9251 Mon. – Fri. 9 a.m. –5 p.m., Sat. – Sun. Noon – 5 p.m.

Check out "See the Sights" pp. 35

Frame Gallery-Wales
A private frame shop and gallery with rotating exhibits. 114 Main St. (B) 822-0496.

Local Color Art Gallery & Store
As part of its continuing effort to promote the arts, The Arts Council of Brazos Valley regularly features exhibitions of Texas art, demonstrations and tours. Park Place Plaza, 2501 Texas Ave. South (CS) 696-2728.

Myra's Gallery & Custom Framing
A gallery and custom frame shop regularly featuring the work of local and regional artists. 404 University Dr. E. (CS) 693-6894.

Page Two Gallery
A frame shop and gallery of primarily local art. Park Place Plaza, 2501 Texas Ave. South (CS) 695-0109.

Wayne Stark University Center Galleries
A gallery with a three month rotation of paintings, sculptures, woodwork and other exhibits. Located on the main floor in the Memorial Student Center on the Texas A&M Campus. 845-8501 Mon. – Fri. 9 a.m. –5 p.m., Sat. – Sun. Noon – 5 p.m.

The Benjamin Knox Gallery
Features the work of local artist Benjamin Knox. Primarily focuses on Aggie and other local subjects. 404 University Dr. E. (CS) 696-5669.

Texas A&M

has the highest full-time undergraduate enrollment in the nation. The 1997/1997 enrollment was 41,461.

The Red Brick Gallery
Timothy Vanya is the artist in residence and one of the owners of this gallery. The Red Brick Gallery features Vanya's work and that of other artists. On the third week of each month the gallery hosts live entertainment. 202 South Bryan (B) 775-3796.

Visual Arts Gallery
This student-run gallery features the work of a variety of artists. The exhibits change every three months. Located on the second floor in the Memorial Student Center on the Texas A&M Campus 845-9251.

Performing Arts

Aggie Players
The official production company of Texas A&M's theater department. Plan an enjoyable evening watching some of Texas' best young performers. Call the MSC Box office at 845-1234 for information and tickets.

Brazos Valley Symphony Orchestra
A talented class of local performers present a variety of musical styles. Call 774-2877 for information and tickets.

MSC OPAS
World-class performances highlight every OPAS season. The Royal Philharmonic Orchestra, the Prague Chamber Orchestra and Marvin Hamlisch are examples of the high caliber of offered through OPAS. Broadway plays, opera, dance and even something for the kids – OPAS Jr., helps to round out every season. Call the MSC Box Office at 845-1234 for information and tickets.

Stage Center
Talented local performers are featured in Bryan-College Station's oldest community theater. The productions vary from comedy to drama. 701 N. Main (B) 823-4297.

University Chamber Series Music Program
Faculty, students and the community are invited to this weekly series of "Brown Bag" concerts at Texas A&M. For information call the MSC Box Office at 845-1234.

Check out "See the Sights" p. 35

◆◆◆◆◆◆◆

Bryan-College Station Climate Stats

Average Annual Rainfall	39.1 inches
Average January Minimum Temperature	39° F
Average July Maximum Temperature	94° F
Average Growing Season	274 Days
Average Date of First Frost	November 30
Average Date of Last Frost	March 1

Day Trips

There's no need to spend all of your leisure time cooped up in a car searching for a change of pace. Within an hour's drive you can stroll through an antique rose garden, learn about Texas history or witness your favorite flavor of ice cream being made.

A variety of fun and interesting places are located just a stone's throw away from Bryan-College Station. Even long-time residents might uncover a few surprises in this chapter, which is dedicated to getting visitors and newcomers out-and-about.

So, gas up the truck and get ready for a day trip full of more fun than miles!

Anderson

Established in 1834, Anderson's historical main street includes a Victorian courthouse built in 1891.

The courthouse was recently a focal point for a made-for-TV movie directed by Goldie Hawn. The film, titled "Hope," featured many locals as "extras" and was broadcast on TNT in October, 1997.

After looking around Main Street, check out the **Fanthorp Inn State Historical Park**.

Originally of log construction, the Inn was a popular stop for weary stagecoach travelers. Some accounts even have Robert E. Lee, Stonewall Jackson, Sam Houston, Anson Jones and Jefferson Davis as having stayed at the Inn.

Tours Wed. – Sun. 9 a.m. – 4 p.m. On Main Street south of the courthouse. Admission.

Brenham

The original boundaries of Washington County as organized in 1837, included all or parts of Burleson, Lee, Washington and Brazos Counties. Territorial division resulted in the county seat being moved from Washington-on-the-Brazos to Brenham.

Today, some of the earliest homes and most interesting attractions in Texas stand in Brenham.

Take a tour of the **Blue Bell Creamery** which cranks out what many believe is the best ice cream in the country. A 40-minute tour begins with a brief film showing the history of the of "The Little Creamery in Brenham," and ends with a scoop of your favorite flavor. Call 1-800-327-8135 or (409) 830-2197 for tour information. Reservations are required during Spring break.

The **Monastery of St. Clare**, is home to a group of Franciscan Poor Clare Nuns and the Miniature Horses that they raise to support themselves. Visitors are welcome to pet the horses, browse in the gift shop featuring the Nun's handiwork or spend a few moments in the Monastery chapel. Open Mon.-Sun. 2pm-4pm year-round except during Holy Week and on Christmas day. (409) 836-96552. Located 9 miles east of Brenham on State Highway 105.

The **Brenham Heritage Museum** has permanent exhibits that illustrate the history of Brenham and Washington County. Special exhibits are presented throughout the year. Be sure to see the wonderful Silsby Steam Fire Engine on display next door to the museum. The City of Brenham purchased the Silsby in 1879 for $3,000. Wed. 1pm-4pm, Thurs.-

Sat. 10am-4pm. 105 Market Street. (409) 830-8445.

Five acres of greenhouses bursting with lush plants year-round are on the tour at **Ellison's Greenhouses**. Seasonal greenhouses with Easter lilies, poinsettias, tulips and hydrangeas are awash in holiday color when the flowers bloom. Mon. – Sat. 9:30am-5:00pm. Tourist center and gift shop at 1808 S. Horton while the greenhouse entrance is at 2107 E. Stone St. (409) 836-6011.

Plan some extra time to discover the many antique and specialty shops in downtown Brenham.

Caldwell

The City of Caldwell is named for Mathew "Old Paint" Caldwell, an Indian Fighter who saw action against Santa Anna near San Antonio. Founded in 1840, Caldwell is known today as the "Kolache Capital of Texas."

The **Burleson County Czech Heritage Museum** provides insight and information on the Czech history, culture and heritage. Exhibits include Czech costumes, crystals, books and other items. 212 W. Buck St. (Located in the Chamber of Commerce building).

Learn about local history at the **Burleson County Historical Museum**. The collection includes many fascinating early artifacts and an exhibit that tells the story of Fort Tenoxtitlan. Established by Mexico in 1830 to discourage a colonial uprising, the fort's commander

50

Beautiful Brazos River

eventually joined the fight for Texas' independence – on the side of the colonists. The commander is said to be one of the signers of the Texas Declaration of Independence. Fri. 2-4:30pm. Located at the Burleson County Courthouse.

Calvert

Admire the Victorian architecture, browse through a specialty shop or search for a one-of-a-kind piece in one of the many antiques stores lining Main Street. Known as the "Antique Capital of Texas," the entire town has been designated a National Historic District. Not surprisingly, Calvert is packed with homes and buildings dating from 1868 to the early 1900s. Located about 30 miles North of Bryan on Texas 6, Calvert is a must for enthusiasts of antiques, art or architecture.

Chapel Hill

Established in 1847, Chapel Hill was once a bustling cultural and educational center. Today, charming shops and historical buildings dot Main Street.

Take a walking tour through downtown to view the many early Texas and ante-bellum structures. Stop in at the **Chapel Hill Bank**, chartered in 1907. Still in its original location, the bank is the oldest continuously operated bank in Texas. Many original photos, documents and relics remain from the early days.

The **Chapel Hill Historical Society Museum** houses photos, documents and other items that chronicle the history of the town. Once the site of the former Chapel Hill Female College, the museum provides insight into the life and times of the town's pioneer settlers. Wed.-Sat. 10am-4pm; Sun. 1pm-4pm. (409) 836-6033.

Independence

Originally named Coles Settlement in 1824, the town was founded by John P. Coles, one of Stephen F. Austin's "First Three Hundred" families in Texas. In 1836, the town was renamed "Independence" to commemorate the state's independence from Mexico. Several noteworthy attractions call Independence home.

Initially the site of the historic Hairston-McKnight homestead, the **Antique Rose Emporium** features a number of display gardens with herbs, native plants and "living antique roses." The antique roses at the Emporium are descendants of 2,000 year-old plants. Open Tues.-Sat. 9am-6pm; Sun. 11am-5:30pm. Located on F.M. 50, just south of the F.M. 390 intersection.

The Independence Baptist Church and Museum, organized in 1839, is the oldest continual Baptist church in Texas. In 1845, the church established Baylor University for men and women. Open May through February, Wed. – Sat. 10am-4pm. In March and April, Mon.-Sat. 10am-4pm. Located at 10405 FM 50. (409) 836-5117.

Plantersville

Founded in 1885, Plantersville was located along the Colorado & Santa Fe Railroad. Wagon making and agriculture were dominant industries until the late 1800s. Today, the town

> ### FYI
> The Texas Renaissance Festival in Plantersville is held on seven weekends in the fall (Oct. – Nov.) Call (409) 894-2516 for information.

is best known for fresh fruit and the Texas Renaissance Festival.

Spend a cool Texas morning **at The King's Orchard** picking strawberries, blackberries, raspberries, blueberries, peaches, nectarines, plums or apples. From Mar.-Sept., enjoy a picnic lunch and show the kids where fruit really comes from. Call (409) 894-2766 for hours, directions and fruit availability. Located off F.M. 1774 south of Plantersville.

Navasota

Settled as early as 1822, Navasota wasn't officially established until 1859 as a result of the Houston & Texas Central Railroad expansion.

The downtown area is listed on the National Register of Historic homes – an ideal setting for the town's many antique and specialty shops.

The **Horlock History Center** is located in a two-story Eastlake house built in 1892. The three-room collection is devoted to the understanding and celebration of the ethnic diversity of the area. Open Fri. and Sat. 9:30am-4:30pm; Sun. 1pm-4pm. 1215 E. Washington St. (Texas 105).

Washington-on-the-Brazos

Washington-on-the-Brazos State Historical Park is the site of the signing of the Texas Declaration of Independence on March 2, 1836.

Today, the park encompasses **Barrington**, the plantation built in 1844-1845 by Anson Jones, the last president of the Republic of Texas and the **Star of the Republic Museum** which chronicles the history of the Texas Republic through a variety of multi-media exhibits.

The state park has picnic facilities, a playground and an amphitheater. Look for the Independence Monument at the site of Independence Hall.

The park is open daily from 8:00am-sundown and is available for day use only. Barrington is open daily, 10am-5pm. The Star of the Republic Museum is open daily 10am-5pm. Admission. Located on the Brazos River on FM 1155. (409) 878-2461.

Park It!

Imagine rushing down a wet and wild waterslide, watching 50 turtles swim for the bread you've just tossed in the pond, sailing on a clear blue lake or seeing an armadillo scamper across the trail just up ahead of you. All of these and more are possible if you take advantage of Bryan-College Station's 50-plus city parks comprised of over 2,000 acres of prime recreational real estate.

All city parks are open to the public throughout the year and offer a variety of out-door activities. So, whether you prefer a nature hike, fishing or playing sand volleyball, there is a park waiting for you! Best of all, use of most area park facilities are free! Reasonable fees are charged for entrance to swimming pools, use of pavilions and day use and camping at Lake Bryan.

In addition to providing the space and facilities for running, swimming and picnicking, the Bryan-College Station Parks Departments offer a number of programs for the young and the young at heart. Basketball, flag football, volleyball, softball, tennis, swimming and other camps, lessons and competitions keep residents fit while they're having fun. Movies, concerts and special events are often held in the city parks so watch the newspaper and listen to the radio for announcements.

Bryan parks are open to the public from 9:30 a.m. until 1:00 a.m. daily. College Station parks are closed daily during the curfew hours of 1:00 a.m. to 5:00 a.m. Alcoholic beverages are prohibited in the parks and open fires are permitted only in designated areas. All litter should be placed in trash containers. It is unlawful to cut or destroy park plants or to swim in the ponds. Pets must be kept on a leash. There are no "off-road" vehicles allowed on park trails and all vehicles should be parked in designated areas. Visitors must obey all official park signs. Firearms, airguns, crossbows and bows and arrows are prohibited. Golfing or driving golf balls in the parks isn't allowed. A current fishing license is required to fish in public parks. All park wildlife is protected.

Bryan-College Station is proud of the number and diversity of its parks and programs. So, what are you waiting for? Check out the detailed listing below and get out and park it!

Bryan Parks

Astin Recreational Area
12 acres: Pavilion, picnic tables, BBQ grills, restrooms, ¼ mile walking trail, gazebo, and pier overlooking the lake with ample parking. 129 Roundtree.

Bonham Park
12 acres: Picnic tables, BBQ grills, playground, 4/10 mile walking trail, basketball and tennis courts, soccer fields, back stops and restrooms. 2315 Russell Street.

Bryan Aquatic Center
3 acres: Heated swimming pool, wading pool, waterslide, BBQ grills and picnic tables. 3100 Oak Ridge Drive.

Bryan High School Tennis Courts
2 acres: Tennis courts. 3401 E. 29th Street.

Bryan Regional Athletic Complex
89 acres: Pavilion, restrooms, nature trail, playground, tennis courts, soccer fields, tennis courts, basketball court, softball fields and Little League fields. 5440 N. Texas Ave.

Camelot Park
Twenty-one acres: Undeveloped with benches and a 4/10-mile interpretive trail. Camelot Drive.

FYI

For more information on local parks call the Bryan Parks Dept. at 361-3656 or the College Station Parks Dept. at 764-3773

Castle Heights Park
7 acres: Picnic tables, BBQ grills, playground, restrooms and basketball court. 1501 Hooper Street.

Copperfield Park
6 acres: Pavilion, picnic tables, BBQ grills, tennis court, playground, sand volleyball and wooded area. 4521 Canterbury Drive.

Crescent Park
2 acres: Undeveloped except for a backstop. The park features beautiful Spring wildflowers. 401 Hensel Avenue.

Garden Acres
1 acre: Undeveloped with colorful wildflowers in the springtime. 9745 Garden Acres Blvd.

Sue Haswell Park
19 acres: Swimming pool, pavilion with a kitchen, picnic tables, BBQ grills, restroom, playground, swimming pool, tennis courts, softball fields, basketball court, sand volleyball court and horseshoe pits. 1142 E. William Joe Bryan.

Henderson Park
22 acres: Pavilion, picnic tables, BBQ grills, restrooms, playground and basketball court. 1629 Mockingbird Rd. Lane.

See "Day Trips" p. 49

education
fitness
games
crafts
sports
classes

Neal Recreation Center
Bryan Parks and Recreation
600 Randolph – Bryan

Heritage Park
2.5 acres: Historical park. The gazebo is a favorite spot for prom and wedding pictures. 200 E. 31st Street.

Jane Long School Park
26 acres: Picnic tables, BBQ grills, tennis courts, soccer fields, fitness area, football field, track, softball backstops and a 6/10-mile-jogging trail. 439 S. FM 2818.

Lake Bryan Park
840 acres: Pavilion, picnic tables, BBQ grills, playground, horseshoe pits, outdoor shower, swimming area, fishing, fishing dock, boating, boat ramp, jet ski area, primitive and developed camping sites with water and electricity. Day use and camping fee. 8200 Sandy Point Road/FM 1687.

> **FYI**
> The best park to see and feed turtles at is Astin Park in Bryan.

Lyons
1 acre: Undeveloped with picnic tables and playground. Adjacent to Bonham Park.

Municipal Golf Course
125 acres: Golf, pond, kitchen, restrooms. 206 W. Villa Maria Road.

Neal Park
2 acres: Recreation center, picnic tables, BBQ grills, playground and basketball court. 500 North Randolph.

Redbud Park
Landscaped open playing area. 210 Redbud Street.

Sadie Thomas Park
129 acres: Swimming pool, pavilions, playground, soccer field, softball field, covered multi-use basketball court. 129 Moss Street.

Sam Rayburn School Park
24 acres: Picnic tables, BBQ grills, playground, tennis courts, covered multi-use basketball court, football stadium, track, softball backstops, soccer fields, 6/10 of a mile walking trail, and wheelchair fitness course. 1449 East Bypass.

Photo: City of Bryan
Enjoying a cool afternoon at the park

San Jacinto School Park
2 acres: Pavilion, picnic tables, BBQ grill, playground, basketball court and backstop. 1503 Saunders Street.

Scurry Park
7 acres: Pavilion, picnic tables, BBQ grills, playground, basketball court and restrooms. 1501 Wellington Street.

Tanglewood Park
19 acres: Pavilion, picnic tables, BBQ grills, playground, tennis courts, soccer fields, volleyball court and restrooms. 3900 Carter Creek Pkwy.

Villa West
10 acres: Undeveloped on Villa Maria West Road behind Mary Branch School Elementary School.

Washington
1 acre: Picnic tables, and playground. 500 E. 20th St.

Williamson
10 acres: Pavilion, BBQ grills, picnic tables, Playground, restrooms, tennis and basketball court. 411 Williamson Drive.

College Station Parks
Anderson
8.9 acres: Pavilion, playground, jogging trail, restrooms, basketball court and soccer fields. 900 Anderson.

Arboretum
17 acres: Pavilion, pond and nature trails. 1900 Anderson.

Bee Creek
26.5 acres: Swimming pool, pavilion, restrooms, picnic tables, playground, nature trails, softball fields, tennis courts and volleyball court. 1900 Anderson.

Brison
9.2 acres: Open play area and jogging trail. 400 Dexter Drive.

Brothers Pond
16.1 acres: Pavilion, picnic tables, playground, pond, nature trails, jogging trail and basketball court. 3100 Rio Grande.

Central
47.2 acres: Pavilion, restrooms, picnic tables, tree-shaded playground, pond, nature trail, basketball court, soccer fields, softball fields, tennis courts and volleyball court. 1000 Krenek Tap Rd.

Cy Miller
2.5 acres: Pavilions, picnic tables, fishing pond, jogging trail. 2615 Texas Ave.

Eastgate
1 acre: Open play area. 903 Foster, & Walton at Texas Ave.

Edelweiss
10.9 acres: Undeveloped. Victoria Ave.

Emerald Forest
4.5 acres: Picnic tables, playground, nature trail, jogging trail and basketball court. 8400 Appomattox.

Gabba Rd.
10.7 acres: Pavilion, picnic tables, playground, pond, and jogging trail. 1201 Dexter Dr. South.

George K. Fitch
11.3 acres: Pavilion, picnic tables, playground, nature trail and basketball court. 1100 Balcones.

Hensel TAMU
29.7 acres: Pavilion, restrooms, picnic tables, playground, nature trail, fitness court and volleyball court. College Ave.

Jack & Dorothy Miller
10 acres: Pavilion, picnic tables, playground, jogging trail, basketball courts and soccer fields. 501 Rock Prairie Rd.

Lemontree
15.4 acres: Picnic tables, playground, nature trail, jogging trail, basketball court and softball fields. 1300 Lemontree Drive.

Lick Creek
515.5 acres: Undeveloped with walking trails, pond, wildflowers and great wildlife viewing. East Rock Prairie.

Lincoln Center at W.A. Tarrow Park
8 acres: Recreation center with volleyball, basketball, playground, jogging trail, soccer fields and restrooms. 1000 Eleanor.

Lions

1.5 acres: Picnic tables, playground and basketball court. 501 Chapel.

Longmire

4.2 acres: picnic tables. 2600 Longmire Drive.

Luther Jones

1.8 acres: Open play area – neighborhood park. 501 Park Place.

Merry Oaks

4.6 acres: Picnic tables, playground, nature trail, jogging trail and basketball court. 1401 Merry Oaks Drive.

Oaks

7.5 acres: Pavilion, picnic tables, jogging trail, basketball court and restrooms. 1601 Stallings.

Parkway

1.9 acres: Picnic tables and playground. 901 Woodland Parkway.

Pebble Creek

10.2 acres: Pavilion, playground, jogging trail, basketball court and soccer fields. 401 Parkview.

Raintree

13 acres: Pavilion, picnic tables, playground, nature trail, jogging trail and volleyball court. 2505 Raintree Drive.

Richard Carter

7.4 acres: Historical site with open play areas and nature trail. 1800 Brazoswood.

Sandstone

15 acres: Pavilion, playground, jogging trail, basketball court and soccer fields. 1700 Sebesta Rd.

Southwood

44.7 acres: Swimming pool, pavilion, playground, restrooms, basketball courts, soccer fields, softball fields, tennis courts, volleyball court and swimming pool. 1600 Rock Prairie Rd.

Thomas

16.1 acres: Swimming pool, pavilion, picnic tables, playground, jogging trail, fitness courts, basketball courts, soccer fields, tennis courts and swimming pool. 1300 James Parkway.

Wayne Smith Park

2.0 acres: Pavilion, playground, and picnic tables and basketball court. 401 Luther.

Wayne Smith Ball Fields

10.8 acres: Pavilions, restrooms and softball fields. Wellborn & Holleman to be completed Spring of 1999.

Windwood

1 acre: Playground and picnic tables. 2650 Brookway.

Wolf Pen Creek

19.47 acres: Pavilion, playground, picnic tables, restrooms, pond, jogging trail and amphitheater. 1015 Colgate.

Woodcreek

6.6 acres: Playground, picnic tables, nature trail, jogging trail and basketball court. 9100 Shadowcrest Drive.

FYI

Many area parks have barbecue pits and tables. Why not take a picnic dinner and spend the day at the park?

**Check out
"See the Sights" p. 60**

Family Pak

The days of the home-based birthday party may be behind us, figuring out how to get the kids away from the TV is tough, and finding something fun for the entire family to do together is nearly impossible! Well, in this chapter you might just find some solutions to these family dilemmas.

Bryan-College Station is family-friendly with a variety of things to do and see. Everything from birthday parties to tennis is covered in this chapter. Peruse the entries here, and then check out the "See the Sights" and "Day Trips" chapters for more family fun!

City Swimming Pools

Bryan-College Station has plenty of city pools to keep you cool this summer. The pool season runs May through September, except where noted. Admission fees vary – usually between $1.75 and $3.25 per swim. So, check out these swimming holes – they're a splash!

Adamson Lagoon
Seasonal, 1900 Anderson, Bee Creek Park, (CS) 764 –3735.

Bryan Aquatic Center
Heated year-round, 3100 Oak Ridge (B), 361-3650.

Hallaran Pool
Seasonal, 1600 Rock Prairie Rd., Southwood Park, (CS) 764-3738.

Haswell Pool
Seasonal, 505 N. Coulter (B) 361-3651.

Natatorium at College Station Jr. High School
Limited hours during school year, 900 Rock Prairie Rd. (CS) 764-5554.

Sadie Thomas Pool
200 Moss St. (B) 361-3654.

Thomas Pool
1300 James Parkway, Thomas Park, (CS) 764-3721.

Golf

Rain, shine or hot, dry weather – it doesn't matter – some people insist on chasing a small ball around just to hit it into a hole. The odds are against them, the obstacles insurmountable but these people never give up. We call these stout-hearted, dedicated folks - golfers

Players of all abilities will find a course or practice range to suit their style in Bryan-College Station. Greens fees, tee times, and availability of carts vary, so be sure to call ahead.

A&M Golf Course
Open to public, Par 70 course. Texas A&M University Campus (CS) 845-1723.

The Big Hit Driving Range
3715 Mohawk (B) 776-0300.

FYI

The Toy Library in Bryan lends toys to area families. Call 693-3697.

Briarcrest Country Club
Membership only, Par 72 course. 1929 Country Club Dr. (B) 776-0133.

Bryan Municipal Golf Course
Open to public, Par 70 course. Villa Maria and South College (B) 823-0126.

Department of Recreational Sports Golf Driving Range
Texas A&M University Campus (CS) 845-7826.

Greensworld Par 3 Golf Course
Lighted course. 1005 E. Texas Bypass 6 (CS) 764-0596.

Pebble Creek Golf Course
Semi-private, Par 72 course. 4500 Pebble Creek Parkway (CS) 690-0990.

Tennis

Tennis is thriving in Bryan-College Station, but there are plenty of courts for everyone. Players of all abilities put area tennis courts to good use year-round.

The parks and recreation departments offer tennis classes and league play for players of all ages. So, whether you play for the fun or competition, grab a racket and head to the nearest court.

Bee Creek Park Courts
1900 Anderson (CS).

Central Park Courts
1000 Krenek Tap Rd. (CS).

Oaks Park Courts
1601 Stallings (CS).

Sadie Thomas Park Courts
129 Moss St. (B).

Southwood Athletic Park Courts
1600 Rock Prairie Rd. (CS).

Sue Haswell Park Courts
1142 E. William Joe Bryan (B).

Tanglewood Park
3900 Carter Creek Parkway (B).

Thomas Park
1300 James Parkway (CS).

Williamson Park
411 Williamson Dr. (B).

FYI

The College Station Parks Department offers a variety of fun classes for the whole family. Take tennis, creative writing, cooking and more! Call 764-3486

Bowling

MSC Bowling and Games
Eight bowling lanes, ten pool tables coin operated or by the hour, and video games. Located in the MSC on the Texas A&M Campus. Mon. – Fri. 8 a.m. – midnight; Sat. 9 a.m. – midnight; Sun. 1:30 p.m. – midnight. (CS) 862-2429.

Triangle Bowl
Home of the only "Glow Bowl" in town where the lights are turned off and black lights and strobes are turned on for an out-of-this-world atmosphere. The center has 28 lanes, video games and darts. Leagues and open bowling. 3810 Old College Rd. (B) 846-8761 Mon. – Fri. 9 a.m. – 12 a.m., Sat. noon – 1 a.m., Sun. noon – 12 a.m. Summer hours vary.

Wolf Pen Bowling Center
Featuring 40 lanes plus video games. League and open bowling. 2400 E. Bypass (CS) 696-1100. Mon.-Fri. 8 a.m. – 11, Sat. - Sun. noon- 11:30 p.m.

Skating

Wolf Pen Skate

Roller skating fun for the whole family, pool tables and video games. Admission includes skate rental. 2400 E. Bypass (CS) 693-8099 Mon.-Thurs. 10 a.m. – 10 p.m., Fri. – Sat. 10 to midnight, Sun 1 p.m. – 8 p.m.

Mini-Golf

Putt Putt Golf, softball and baseball batting cages, bumper boats and video games provides fun for all ages. 1705 Valley View (CS) 693-2445 Mon. – Thurs. 9 a.m. – midnight, Fri. – Sat. 9 a.m. – 1 a.m., Sun. 11 a.m. – 11 p.m.

Photos: City of Bryan
At parties or at play... there's a lot for kids to do in Bryan-College Station!

Party Central

Every birthday is special, but if you want it to be extra special – check out one of these local party haunts. The kids in your life will thank you!

With plenty to keep youngsters busy and prices ranging from $50 to $100 for a party with up to ten children, these business offer birthday bashes that are both easy on the carpet and on your wallet!

Adamson Lagoon

Theme parties are all the rage at this local water park. Pick a theme and party at the pool between May and September. The party plans vary depending upon the theme but they all include lots of swimming and splashing. 1900 Anderson, Bee Creek Park 764-3773.

Brazos Valley Natural History

Get your kids back to nature on with a theme birthday party at the BVNH. 3232 Briarcrest Drive (B) 776-2195.

Jacque's Toys and Books

Fun and fancy theme parties are on the menu in Jacques party room. 4301A S Texas Ave. (B) 846-8660.

McDonalds

Three of the golden arches deliver extra birthday fun with happy meals and a playground. 825 Villa Maria (B) 822-3011; 2420 Texas Ave. (B) 696-9346; 700 South Texas Av. 822-1548.

Mr. Gatti's

Kids love having birthday parties here! Who wouldn't want to eat pizza, guzzle coke, play arcade games, ride bumper cars and climb around on a huge jungle gym? 1673 Briarcrest Dr. (B) 731-8646.

The Party Park

Have a birthday carnival at Mike Ormsby's place. With Carnival rides, clowns, balloons and party games the kids are sure to have a blast! 3610 Shirley Dr. Bryan 778-3388.

Power Kids

Give that computer whiz just what she's always wanted – a high tech birthday party. Kids get to use their favorite software and multimedia titles. The parties are a mixture of new-age fun, entertainment and education. 2418-D South Texas Ave. (CS) 696-5743.

Texas A&M MSC

Texas A&M students, faculty and staff can book a party at the MSC. Enjoy bowling, video games, shooting pool and more. For groups from 12 to 112, the MSC is a classy place to party. Call the MSC Party Hot Line 862-2429.

TJ Laser Tag
Laser tag, video games, food and fun are in the party plan at TJ's Laser Tag. Kids and adults will have a blast! 315 South College (CS) 846-6040.

Putt Putt Golf and Games
Putt Putt Golf, softball and baseball batting cages, bumper boats and video games provides party fun for all ages. 1705 Valley View (CS) 693-2445 Mon. – Thurs. 9 a.m. – midnight, Fri. – Sat. 9 a.m. – 1 a.m., Sun. 11 a.m. – 11 p.m.

Movie Theaters
College Park 6
2080 E. 29th St. 775-2463.

Hollywood 16
1401 Hwy 6 Bypass (CS) 764-7592.

Carmike Theater
Three screens, 1500 Harvey Rd. (CS) 693-2796.

Photo: City of Bryan
Lake Bryan provides fishing, boating and swimming for the whole family!

Book It!

Libraries make an important contribution to the community through special programming, sponsoring speakers and most importantly by bringing the world to our doorstep within the pages of books or through electronic media. With the definition of library services changing rapidly, the options for library research and recreational reading or viewing are expanding.

Bryan-College Station's libraries include tapes, videos and compact disks. Texas A&M libraries even offer Internet access to students. Wouldn't Ben Franklin be surprised to see how his simple notion of a lending library has evolved? Today's library can take you places and teach you things that even Mr. Franklin couldn't have imagined.

Learn about the Australian Outback, the Oregon Coast or a thousand other destinations without ever leaving home. Become more confident, master a new language or learn to laugh a little more often when you take the time to visit a local library. Surely, there is something for everyone.

The libraries are accessible to anyone in Bryan-College Station for research. Check out privileges vary and may be obtained at any of the libraries, except Blinn College. Blinn does not extend circulation privileges to the community at large. Both the George Bush Presidential Library and the Medical Sciences Library on the Texas A&M campus, issue library cards for their specific collections. The Evans Library issues a card valid at all of its branch locations.

Bryan-College Station has several libraries to choose from, each with their own unique collections services and character. Spend a few hours browsing the magazine isle, poking around the fiction stacks or visit the children's section with your own young readers. It will be time well spent!

Bryan Library

This downtown library serves all of Brazos County through a Bookmobile, a branch in College Station and an inter-library loan program with College Station. Offers summer reading programs for children. Open Mon., Tues. and Thurs. 9 a.m. – 9 p.m. and Wed., Fri. and Sat. 9 a.m. – 5 p.m. Closed Sun. 201 E. 26th St. (B) 361-3715.

College Station Library

A bright, well appointed and contemporary building is the new home of the College Station Library. The doors opened in March, 1998 with twice the shelf-space, a children's area with cushioned seating and several meeting rooms. Special summer programming for children, an inter-library loan program with the Bryan Library and other special services are available Open Mon. 10 a.m. – 9 p.m.; Tues. & Thurs. 10 a.m. – 7 p.m.; Wed., Fri. & Sat. 10 a.m. – 5 p.m. Closed Sun. . 800 F.M. 2818 (CS) 764-3416.

Carnegie Library

Bryan-College Station is home to the oldest Carnegie Library building in Texas. The structure was built in 1903 using funds from the Carnegie foundation. The Classic Revival style building was designed by Professor F.E. Gieseck and has in recent years undergone an extensive renovation.

Scheduled for re-opening in the fall of 1998 the library will operate under the Bryan Library System and house collections of Texas history, genealogy, rare books and children's literature. 101 S. Main (B) Call the Bryan Library for hours 361-3715.

Blinn College Library

The Blinn College Library serves its' students, faculty and staff with a collection representative of the academic, allied health and occupational courses offered. 2520 E. Villa Maria Rd. (B) 821-0270. Hours vary.

Sterling C. Evans Library

The Sterling C. Evans is the main library serving the Texas A&M campus. The library includes current periodicals, electronic databases and services, a map library, copy center, NOTIS and more. Located on the

Photo: Rhonda Brinkmann

College Station's spacious new library provides residents with ample room for studying, research or recreational reading

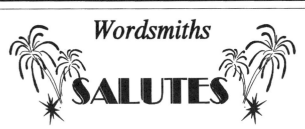
Texas A&M Campus. Hours vary. Call 862-2668 to hear a recording with current hours. Call 845-5741 for information.

Cushing Memorial Library

The Cushing Memorial Library is the rare book, manuscript, research collection and archive repository for Texas A&M University. The holdings include maps, pamphlets, manuscripts, photographs, ephemera, newspapers, government documents and more. Advance notice is required for access to some of the collections, so it is wise to call ahead. Hours vary. Cushing is a branch of the Evans Library. Call 845-1951 for information.

See "Higher Ed"
p. 80

Medical Sciences Library

Medicine and Veterinarian Medicine are the focus of this library's collection. The library is part of the College of Medicine and College of Veterinarian Medicine and is administered separately from the Evans Library. The regulations regarding access to the collection vary from other campus libraries so call for information. Located on West Campus. There is a free inter-campus shuttle available to and from West Campus. Hours vary. Call 845-7427 for information.

West Campus Library

This library houses most of the materials for business and agricultural programs. The library includes the R.C. Barclay Reference and Retailing Resource Center. The West Campus Library is a branch of the Evans Library. Located on West Campus. Hours vary. Call 845-2111 for information.

FYI

A free inter-campus shuttle runs between the main and West campuses.

Poly Sciences and Economics Library (PSEL)

The library includes several hundred journals available electronically in full text format, databases available remotely via personal computer and CD-ROM based information. Recent additions to the collection include: economics working papers. Future expansion plans includes obtaining material from the Top 20 economics departments in the United States. Located on West Campus in the George Bush School of Government and Public Services. Hours vary. Call 862-3544 for information.

George Bush Presidential Library

History will be examined, written and re-written as researchers uncover the depth and breath of President George Bush's public service. The Bush Library has 38,000,000 pages of official and personal papers, 1,000,000 photographs, 2,500 hours of videotape and 50,000 Bush artifacts in its collection. The library is the tenth Presidential Library operated by the National Archives and Records. On-site access to research materials after orientation. - 1000 George Bush Drive, West (CS). For information on research access call 260-9552.

Photo: Rhonda Brinkmann
The George Bush Presidential Library welcomes researchers and visitors

Elementary and Secondary Schools

Bryan-College Station's growing population has caused a dramatic increase in the number of public and private schools. As development swells, pushing the twin cities' boundaries outward, even more campuses will be needed.

Currently, there are 20 public schools in Bryan, 10 public schools in College Station and plans are underway to build additional campuses. Over one dozen private schools compliment the educational opportunities in the twin cities with enrollment for pre-K through 12th grade. In recent years, home schooling has become a popular alternative to campus-based learning.

More than ever before, parents can influence the type of education that their children receive. The opportunity for involvement ranges from volunteering a few hours a week to developing an entire curriculum. These options make education in Bryan-College Station a very personal choice.

Public schools are more uniform in the curriculum that they present, while private and home-based schools have more latitude in choosing an educational approach – be it traditional, moderate or innovative.

Most private schools offer campus tours and will send information upon request. See the listing of private schools at the end of this chapter for more information. Those interested in home-schooling may contact the Brazos Valley Christian Home Educators Association at 696-2651 for information on how to get started or to locate a home educators support group nearby.

The many facets of private schooling make it difficult to summarize in a publication such as this. Therefore, the names, addresses and telephone numbers of area private schools are listed at the end of this chapter. Please contact them directly for further information. The rest of this chapter will focus on public schools.

Academic excellence, student achievement and campus expansions keep Bryan-College Station public schools in the spotlight year-round.

Academic Excellence

Public schools in Texas are accredited by the Texas Education Agency (TEA). Each school district is required to publish an annual report describing the educational performance of individual schools for the previous school year. The TEA ranks schools based upon several factors for the total student population and the following four sub-groups: African American, Hispanic, White and economically disadvantaged. See the table below for the 1998 academic designations and criteria.

Designation	Percent of Total Students and Sub-Groups Passing TAAS	Percent of Total Students and Sub-Groups Missing 12 Days or Less of School	Percent of Total Students and Sub-Groups Dropping Out
Unacceptable	<40%	<94%	6.0 +
Acceptable	At least 40%	At least 94%	6.0 or less
Recognized	At least 80%	At least 94%	3.5% or less
Exemplary	At least 90%	At least 94%	1% or less

Photo: City of Bryan

Area students learn about fire safety

Based upon student performance in 1997-1998, all schools in both districts were academically acceptable at all grade levels. Three College Station and five Bryan elementary schools were ranked even higher.

College Hills and Pebble Creek in College Station, and Johnson and Bowen in Bryan, were rated "Exemplary." South Knoll and Rock Prairie in College Station, and Henderson, Houston and Branch in Bryan, received "Recognized" status.

Excellence in Teaching

High academic ratings are indicative of the standard of excellence set by the faculty and staff in area schools. During the 1997-1998 school year, local teachers garnered a number of honors including: Regional Teacher of the Year, Regional College Board AP Teacher Recognition and the National Science Foundation's Presidential Award for Excellence in the Teaching of Science. It is the professionalism and dedication of our teachers that set the stage for students to excel.

Student Achievement

The students, parents and faculty of the Bryan-College Station schools have a great deal to be proud of. Whether in academics, sports, or the arts, local students consistently stand in the winner's circle.

During the 1997-1998 school year, College Station's Willow Branch Intermediate students took first place at the Sam Rayburn University Interscholastic Tournament. Also, A&M Consolidated High School students earned second place in the Regional U.S. Science Bowl held at Texas A&M University. College Station Junior High band members received a total of 88 "First Division"

Photo: Rhonda Brinkmann
Bowen Elementary School in Bryan welcomes students through its "Gateway to Time" entrance.

awards for solo and/or ensemble performances. Bryan High School's Senior Class is proud of its 16 National Merit students and 22 AP (Advanced Placement) Scholars. Bryan High School's Boys Gymnastics were national champions. And, the list goes on.

The growth in the student population and the trend towards an increasingly diverse curriculum, have driven expansion and improvement initiatives on local campuses.

Campus Expansions

In the past year, both high schools have undergone extensive renovation and expansion. A&M Consolidated High School's new classrooms, gym, library and cafeteria were completed by the first day of classes for the 1998-1999 school year. Bryan High School's immense addition will accommodate the 9th graders from the Lamar Campus beginning with the 1999-2000 school year. The ground breaking for a new intermediate school on Graham Road in College Station took place in Spring, 1998. The middle schools in Bryan are slated for future expansion with new wings on the drawing boards. On-going construction projects at elementary schools include enlarging classrooms, adding special use facilities and building an infrastructure for technology. These projects are an important part of meeting the growing needs of students in both school districts.

Want to Learn More?

Both the Bryan and College Station Independent School Districts will send information about their schools if requested. However, the best way to learn about a school is to check it out for yourself. To that end,

74

we have included detailed information on each public school in the twin cities. Call the principal, visit the campus or better yet, spend some time volunteering in area schools!

Bryan Schools

Bohnham Elementary *(K-5)*
2801 Wilkes Drive
Bryan, TX 77803
361-5370
Principal: Ken Newbold
Enrollment: 512
Mascot: Bucchaneer
Colors: Green, White

Bowen Elementary *(K-5)*
4825 Copperfield
Bryan, TX 77802
731-7550
Principal: Linda Sasse
Enrollment: 370
Mascot: Bobcat
Colors: Burgundy, Hunter Green

Branch Elementary *(K-5)*
2040 West Villa Maria
Bryan, TX 77807
361-5290
Principal: David Ogden
Enrollment: 598
Mascot: Bear
Colors: Red, White, Blue

Carver Early Childhood Center *(Pre-K)*
1401 W. Martin Luther King Jr.
Bryan, TX 77803
361-5336
Principal: Dr. Rhonda Richardson
Enrollment: 418
Mascot: Caterpillar
Colors: Green, Yellow

Crockett Elementary *(K-5)*
401 Elm Street
Bryan, TX 77801

361-5376
Principal: Janet Orme
Enrollment: 418
Mascot: Rockets
Colors: Blue, Gold

Fannin Elementary *(K-5)*
1200 Baker Street
Bryan, TX 77803
361-5380
Principal: Carolyn Taylor
Enrollment: 512
Mascot: Falcon
Colors: Royal Blue, White

Henderson Elementary *(K-5)*
801 Matous Street
Bryan, TX 77802
361-5385
Principal: Doris Ruffino
Enrollment: 388
Mascot: Hawk
Colors: Green, White

Houston Elementary *(K-5)*
4501 Canterbury Drive
Bryan, TX 77802
731-7500
Principal: Pati Caperton
Enrollment: 562
Mascot: Raven
Colors: Royal Blue, White

Johnson Elementary *(K-5)*
3800 Oak Hill Street
Bryan, TX 77802
361-5388
Principal: Carol Happ
Enrollment: 309
Mascot: Jaguar
Colors: Navy Blue, Goldenrod

> **FYI**
> Many area retailers keep detailed lists of the supplies required by school and grade level.

Bowen Elementary School's "Alamo Wall" in the library brings Texas History alive

Jones Elementary *(3-5)*
1400 Pecan Street
Bryan, TX 77803
361-5350
Principal: Dr. Marcia Murray
Enrollment: 505
Mascot: Star
Colors: Blue, White
Special Note: Home of the Bryan Academy for the Visual and Performing Arts.

Kemp Elementary *(K-5)*
1601 W. Martin Luther King Jr. St.
Bryan, TX 77803
361-5360
Principal: Charlie Chatman
Enrollment: 367
Mascot: Cubs
Colors: Maroon, White

Milam Elementary *(K-2)*
1201 Ridgedale Street
Bryan, TX 77803
361-5392
Principal: Frances McArthur
Enrollment: 533
Mascot: Mustang

Colors: Blue, White

Navarro Elementary *(K-5)*
4520 Northwood Drive
Bryan, TX 77803
361-5300
Principal: Judy Joiner
Enrollment: 425
Mascot: Chaparral
Colors: Blue, White

Neal Elementary *(K-5)*
801 W. Martin Luther King Jr. St.
Bryan, TX 77803
821-6600
Principal: Linda Asberry
Enrollment: 452
Mascot: Eagle
Colors: Gold, White

Ross Elementary *(K-5)*
3300 Parkway Terrace
Bryan, TX 77802
361-5394
Principal Diana Landrum
Enrollment: 332
Mascot: Raccoon
Colors: Navy Blue, White

Jane Long Middle School *(6-8)*
449 South FM 2818
Bryan, TX 77803
821-6500
Principal: Ginger Wentrcek
Enrollment: 1,010
Mascot: Lobos
Colors: Red, White

Sam Rayburn Middle School *(6-8)*
1449 South State Hwy. 6
Bryan, TX 77802
731-7600
Principal: Jerry Ellis
Enrollment: 1,114
Mascot: Raiders
Colors: Blue, Gold

Stephen F. Austin *(6-8)*
801 South Ennis
Bryan, TX 77803
821-6700
Principal: Lowell Strike
Enrollment: 1,087
Mascot: Broncos
Colors: Green, White

Bryan High School *(10-12)*
3401 East 29th St.
Bryan, TX 77802
731-7400
Principal: Dr. Joe Kopec
Enrollment: 2,401
Mascot: Viking
Colors: Blue, Silver

**Bryan High School at
Lamar Campus** *(9)*
1901 Villa Maria
Bryan, TX 77802
731-7770
Principal: Sharon Ward
Enrollment: 966
Mascot: Viking
Colors: Blue, Silver

**Hammond-Oliver High School
for the Human Sciences** *(9-12)*
1305 Memorial Drive
Bryan, TX 77802
731-7830
Dean: Judy Hughson
Special Opportunity School (9-12)
2918 N. State Hwy. 6
Bryan, TX 77808
361-5346

**ACE Drop Out Recovery
Program** *(Ages 16-21)*
1307 Memorial Drive
Bryan, TX 77802
731-7855
Dean: Susan Wilson

See "Family Pak" p. 60

College Station Schools
College Hills Elementary *(K-4)*
1101 Williams St.
College Station, TX 77840
764-5565
Principal: Robert Garner
Enrollment: 650
Mascot: Tiger
Colors: Maroon

Pebble Creek Elementary *(Head
Start, K-4)*
200 Parkway Drive
College Station, TX 77845
764-5595
Principal: Dr. Brad Lancaster
Enrollment: 574
Mascot: Panther
Colors: Maroon, White

Rock Prairie Elementary *(K-4)*
3400 Welsh Ave.
College Station, TX 77845
764-5570
Principal: Dr. Nancy Thornberry
Enrollment: 580
Mascot: Ranglers
Colors: Blue, Silver

South Knoll Elementary
(Head Start, Pre-K-4)
1220 Boswell St.
College Station, TX 77840
764-5580
Principal: Terresa Katt
Enrollment: 580
Mascot: Tiger
Colors: Maroon, White

Southwood Valley Elementary
(Head Start, K-4)
2700 Brothers Blvd.
College Station, TX 77845
764-5590
Principal: Starlet Licona
Enrollment: 520
Mascot: Eagle
Colors: Blue

Photo: Rhonda Brinkmann

Bowen's "Castle Gateway" leads to kindergarten and first grade classrooms

Oakwood Intermediate *(5-6)*
106 Holik St.
College Station, TX 77840
764-5530
Principal: Kathryn Johnston
Enrollment: 511
Mascot: Wildcats
Colors: Maroon, White, and Gray

Willow Branch Intermediate *(5)*
105 Holik St.
College Station, TX 77840
764-5574
Principal: Gerald Wynn
Enrollment: 564
Mascot: Wildcats
Colors: Green, White

College Station Junior High
(7-8)
900 Rock Prairie Road

College Station, TX 77845
764-5545
Principal: Alan Stolt
Enrollment: 1,140
Mascot: Cubs, Cats
Colors: Maroon, White

A&M Consolidated High School
(9-12)
701 FM 2818
College Station, TX 77840
764-5500
Principal: Chrissy Hester
Enrollment: 1,881
Mascot: Tiger
Colors: Maroon, Silver

Center for Alternative Learning
(9-12)
105 Timber St.
College Station, TX 77840
764-5540

Principal: Dr. Leslie Schueckler
Enrollment: 80-95
Mascot: None
Colors: Maroon, White

Private Schools

Allen Academy *(Pre-K-12)*
3201 F.M. 158
Bryan, TX 77806
776-0731

Alta Vista Academy *(K-12)*
Grandy Road at Wellborn Hwy.
College Station, TX 77840
695-1919

Brazos Christian School
(Pre-K-11)
3000 W. Villa Maria
Bryan, TX 77807
823-1000

Central Christian School
(Pre-K-K)
600 South Coulter St.
Bryan, TX 77803
779-1591

St. Joseph School *(Pre-K-12th)*
109 North Preston
Bryan, TX 77803
822-6641

St. Michael's Academy *(K-12)*
2500 South College Avenue
Bryan, TX 77801
822-2715

Dayspring Christian School
(Pre-K-12)
4004 North Texas Avenue
Bryan, TX 77805
778-3380

Montessori School House
(Pre-K-K)
2509 Roundtree Street
Bryan, TX 77801
822-5192

Longmire Learning Center
(Pre-K-1st)
2718 Longmire Drive
College Station, TX 77845
764-2718

Keystone Montessori *(Pre-K-2nd)*
2320 East Villa Maria Road
Bryan, TX 77802
823-4751

St. Thomas Church Early Learning Center *(Pre-K-1st)*
906 George Bush Drive
College Station, TX 77840
696-1728

Aggieland Country School
(Pre-K-1st)
1500 Quail Run
College Station, TX 77845
696-1674

Bryan-College Station

was named the third fastest growing U.S. metropolitan area in terms of new job growth for the years 1995 to 2025.
1997-1998 American Almanac of Jobs and Salaries

Higher Ed

Bryan-College Station is proud to call Blinn College and Texas A&M University neighbors. Opportunity for education, enrichment and entertainment abound on both campuses. And, the 50,000 students that attend these schools contribute over $160 million dollars to the local economy. Although this chapter is not intended to provide complete histories, we would be remiss in not providing a little background on these fine schools.

Blinn College

The main campus of Blinn College was founded in 1883 as a Mission Institute, operated in Brenham by the Southern Conference of the Methodist Church. In 1889, the school was renamed in honor of the Rev. Christian Blinn, a New Yorker who donated a large sum of money to the school.

In 1929, Blinn became a junior college and was merged with Southwestern University in Georgetown, Texas in 1931. Four years later, the school became a private nondenominational junior college.

At the urging of local residents,

Blinn began offering classes in Brazos County after Allen Academy stopped offering higher education courses. Blinn's first local campus opened in 1970 with classes being held in several locations throughout Bryan-College Station.

In January 1997, a new Bryan campus was dedicated near the corner of E. 29th St. and Villa Maria Road. Currently, about 7,000 students attend classes on the Bryan campus.

Associate's degrees and certificates of proficiency are awarded in a variety of subjects including accounting, automotive technology, child development, computer networking, criminal justice and business. Programs in several healthcare fields including dental assistant, dental hygienist, nursing, physical therapy assistant and radiology technician prepare students to enter the workforce. Traditional coursework that prepares students to transfer to a four-year college are also offered. In fact, Blinn transfers more students to four-year colleges than any other two-year school in the state!

The local campus features a student center, a library, a Learning Center, and Counseling Services. 2520 E. Villa Maria Rd (B) Information 821-0200.

FYI

Don't be surprised if Texas A&M students greet you on the street or on campus with a "Howdy." It's just one of the many traditions in Aggieland.

Photo: City of Bryan
Opening week of Blinn College's Bryan Campus

Texas A&M

The oldest public university in Texas is home to the "Fighting Texas Aggies."

Established in 1876 as an all-male military school, the campus originally had only 40 students and six faculty.

> **FYI**
> The Reed Arena is a recent addition to the TAMU Campus. This multi-purpose facility can seat up to 12,500. Call 862-7330 to see what is happening at this first-class facility.

Texas A&M has a long history of excellence in teaching, research and public service. Today, this world-class university is one of the few institutions that hold Land Grant, Sea Grant and Space Grant distinctions. As one of the five largest centers for higher education, Texas A&M has over 41,000 students enrolled.

The 5,200-acre campus accommodates students from all 50 states and over 100 foreign countries in the following colleges:

- College of Agriculture and Life Sciences
- College of Architecture
- Lowry Mays College & Graduate School of Business
- College of Education
- Dwight Look College of Engineering
- College of Geoscience
- College of Liberal Arts
- College of Medicine
- College of Science
- College of Veterinary Medicine

In addition, Texas A&M is home to the Research Park, which includes the headquarters of the Ocean Drilling Program, the USDA's Food Safety and Inspection Service and National Training Center and the wave tank for the Offshore Technology Research Center.

The following state agencies are also part of the Texas A&M University System: Texas Agricultural Experiment Station, Texas Agricultural Extension Service, Texas Animal Damage Control Service, Texas Engineering Experiment Station, Texas Engineering Extension Service, Texas Forest Service, Texas Transportation Institute and Texas Veterinary Medical Diagnostic Laboratory.

Photo: Rhonda Brinkmann

A student's journey begins here, at Texas A&M's Administration Building

Senior Tour

If you base it on activity level, it can be pretty difficult to pick out the senior or retired citizens in Bryan-College Station. As a rule, these folks don't sit still for too long.

Local seniors volunteer at the Bush Presidential Library, the Brazos Valley Children's Museum and at area hospitals. They work in our schools, shops and restaurants. Many "retired" citizens focus on new beginnings by starting businesses or organizations that contribute to our city's economy or way of life.

Many seniors write, paint, sing and participate in the arts. They spend their leisure time playing a round of golf, a game of tennis or cooling off at a local swimming pool. Bryan-College Station is an exciting place to retire, it seems that there is always something to do here. Perhaps that is why there are so many organizations dedicated to meeting the needs of seniors living in the twin cities.

Whether it's healthcare, transportation, legal or employment services, there is probably an organization that can help. Below is a list of selected services that can help visitors and residents during their "senior tour."

Special Services

The American Association of Retired Persons

Provides information, education and community services for those persons age 50+. Health services, financial education, employment assistance and a variety of other services are available. Brazos Senior Center, 1402 Bristol (B) 822-6873.

See "Arts and Culture"
p. 45

Area Agency on Aging (AAA)

Provides a variety of information and assistance including dental, nutrition and personal care. 1706 E. 29th St.(B) 775-4244.

Brazos County Community Action Agency (BVCCA)

A non-profit service organization offering health, transportation, nutrition and other programs to local seniors. 504 E. 27th (B) 779-7443.

Department of Human Services (DHS)

Offers several programs covering daycare, homecare and long-term care for seniors. 3000 E. Villa Maria (B) 776-7432.

Elder-Aid

A non-profit volunteer group providing transportation, home repair and other services to the elderly. 779-7250.

Eldercare Locator

A national information and referral service of the U.S. Department of Health and Human Services providing information on local agencies and services including meals, home care, home repair, social activities, legal assistance programs and more. 1-800-677-1116.

Elderly/Disabled Energy Assistance

A needs-based program designed to help pay energy bills for households with members 60 years or older. 1720B S. Texas Ave. Suite 205, (B) 779-7407.

Adult Day Care
Community Care for Aged & Disabled (Texas Department of Human Services)

Sponsors a variety of daycare and homecare programs including adult fostercare, Meals on Wheels, and residential care for those who require 24 hour-care. 776-1510.

The Pines Adult Day Center

Provides a variety of activities, health services and transportation. 100 W. Brookside (B) 268-7538.

Sherwood Gardens Adult Day Care Center

Provides daily activities, health monitoring, community outings, physical therapy and transportation. 1401 Memorial Dr. (B) 776-7521.

Continuing Education

55 Alive/Mature Driving AARP

Drivers aged 55+ may enroll for a refresher course for the road. 279-5420.

Elderhostel

An educational travel program for persons 60 and over. Provides low cost travel and non-credit courses. (617) 426-7788.

Talking Book Program – Texas State Library

Loans books and magazines on cassette, in large print and in Braille to the visually impaired. 1-800-252-9605.

Job Opportunities

Senior Texas Employment Program

Provides funding for seniors 60+ to work for non-profit organizations. 1-800-728-2592.

Senior Centers

Brazos County Senior Center

1402 Bristol (B) 822-6873.

College Station Senior Center

1000 Eleanor St. (CS) 764-3750.

Volunteer Opportunities

Retired Senior Volunteer Program of the Brazos Valley (RSVP)

Part of the National Senior Services Corps. This organization matches volunteers with meaningful opportunities for service in non-profit organizations. 775-8111.

Photo: Manor East Mall

Seriors participate in the Senior Games which are sponsored annually by Manor East Mall

Here's to Your Health

Bryan-College Station residents and visitors can rest easier knowing that high quality, affordable medical care is available. With two hospitals, a handful of clinics and a variety of specialty medical centers, the twin cities serve patients throughout the region.

Although the hospitals have limited ambulance service, most patients rely on one of the privately owned ambulance companies for emergency and non-emergency transport. Air ambulance transport is available from AAA Advanced Air Ambulance (800-633-3590), a national service headquartered in Miami, Florida.

The emergency number to call in Bryan-College Station is "911". For a complete listing of medical doctors, health services and specialty medical centers, consult the local telephone book.

Hospitals

College Station Medical Center

This 119-bed, state-of-the-art, facility is the center for more than 40 medical specialties including primary and emergency care, cardiovascular surgery, trauma, respiratory, pulmonary and more. Founded in 1931, the hospital is now part of the Columbia Healthcare System. 1604 Rock Prairie Road (CS) 764-5100.

St. Joseph Regional Health Center

The Health Center is a modern, 210-bed hospital facility that offers complete services from birthing to geriatrics and almost every specialty in between. Specialized units such as the Cancer Center, comprehensive cardiology services, women's services, diagnostic imaging, and rehabilitation services compliment the hospital's primary care, emergency, inpatient surgery, outpatient surgery and critical care units. This non-profit facility has served the Brazos Valley for over 125 years. 2801 Franciscan Drive (B) 776-3777.

Medical Clinics

Care Plus
2411 Southwest Parkway. Suite "B" (CS) 696-0683.

Family Health Clinic
3400 Texas Ave. (B) 268-555.

Scott and White
1600 University Drive E. (CS) 691-3300.

Texas Avenue Medical Clinic
401 S. Texas Ave. (B) 779-4756.

FYI
Dial "911" for emergencies

See "Senior Tour"
p. 83

Texas A&M

has one of the largest campuses in the nation with 5,200 acres of land valued at over one billion dollars.

Get me to the Church

In 1821, Stephen Austin established settlements in Texas with the "First Three Hundred" families at Columbus and Washington-on-the-Brazos. In the face of a law requiring all citizens of Mexico, even colonists, to practice Catholicism, Austin permitted religious freedom tempered by tolerance. Bryan-College Station, yesterday and today, reflects and fosters this attitude.

With over 100 houses of worship and more than 30 denominations, religion is a significant social and cultural force in our community. Local congregations sponsor revivals, picnics, touring speakers, musicals, and other programs covering a wide range of needs and interests. Even non-church members take advantage of the moms-day-out, vacation bible school, weight loss and pre-school programs offered by area churches. There are many churches and programs to choose from – and the list is growing.

Several churches were in the planning stage or under construction at the time of this writing. Additionally, many congregations lacking a facility of their own meet in school gyms, share space in other churches or gather in other multi-purpose buildings. For this reason, it is nearly impossible to include all area congregations – though we've done our level best.

Most churches have services throughout the week and welcome visitors and newcomers. Many churches operate pre-school and mother's day out programs during the week. We have tried to note the churches that offer these programs. The notation "PS" means Pre-school and "MDO" means Mothers Day Out.

Keep an eye out for up-to-date church information in the *Eagle* newspaper, *The Press* and in other community publications.

Assembly of God

Abundant Life Assembly of God, 105 W. 32nd. 822-4508.

Bethel Temple Assembly of God, 2608 E. Villa Maria Blvd. 776-4835.

College Heights Assembly of God, 4100 Old College Rd. 846-2777.

Templo Buenas Nuevas Spanish Assembly of God, 1206 San Jacinto Ln., 823-7035.

Baha'i

The Baha'i Faith, 3205 Coastal Dr. 693-6789..

Baptist

The Baptist movement in Texas dates back to 1837 in Texas when the first missionary Baptist church was established at Washington-on-the-Brazos. This lone church sent out an appeal to Brethren throughout the United States - "come over into Macedonia and help us!" Their plea was answered and by 1860, there were about 500 Baptist churches throughout the state.

Beacon Baptist, 2001 E. Villa Maria Rd. 776-1337.

Bethel Baptist, at Texas 30 & FM 158, 776-8818.

Brazos Baptist, 2511 S. Texas Ave. 779-6189.

Calvary Baptist, 2015 Cavitt Ave. 822-3579.

> **FYI**
> Most local churches welcome visitors and newcomers. Call to find out when services and other gatherings are held.

Central Baptist, 600 S. Coulter Dr. 779-1591.

Christ's Holy Missionary, 1119 Arizona St. 764-1090

Clayton Baptist, 7664 Old Jones Rd. 846-4947

College Station Baptist, 2555 Texas Ave. S. 693-8564

Emmanuel Baptist, 408 E. 24th, 822-1998.

Fellowship Freewill Baptist, 1228 W. Villa Maria Rd. 779-2297.

First Baptist of Bryan, 200 S. Texas Ave. 779-2434. PS

First Baptist of College Station, 2300 Welsh, 696-7000. PS & MDO

Galilee Baptist, 804 N. Logan Ave. 822-2475.

Greater Hope Baptist, 1524 E. 21st. 775-4601.

Hillcrest Baptist, 4220 FM 158, 776-5731.

Morning Star Baptist, 2224 E. Martin L. King, 8223-6981.

Mt. Zion Baptist, RFD 1, 778-9878.

New Birth Baptist Temple, 300 Waco, 822-0045.

New Chapel Baptist, 409 W. 21st. 823-7307.

New Testament Missionary, 1218 Eureka, 822-7940.

New Zion Missionary, 1505 E. 21st. 823-7766.

North Bryan Baptist, 4605 N. Hwy 6, 778-3310.

Northview Baptist, 1809 Tabor Rd. 778-0014.

Parkway Baptist, 1501 Southwest Pkwy. 693-4701.

Peaceful Rest Baptist, 1409 Congo, 822-3628.

Pleasant Grove Baptist, 1401 Juniper, 775-1964.

Pleasant Grove Baptist, 310 M L King W. 822-0595.

Primera Iglesia Bautista, 1009 N. Sims Ave. 822-2773.

Rock Prairie Baptist, 2405 Rock Prairie Rd. 690-8412.

St. Mark Baptist, 6906 Raymond Stotzer Pkwy. 268-1525.

St. Matthews Baptist, 409 Holleman Dr. 696-8468.

Shiloh Baptist, 502 M L King E. 823-5002.

Southern Oaks Baptist, 4301 Carter Creek Pkwy. 846-4042.

Tabernacle Baptist, 907 Florida, 822-0039.

Templo Bautista Emmanuel, 120 Bois D' Arc, 822-6428.

Texas Avenue Baptist, 3400 Texas Ave. S. 696-6000.

Trinity Baptist, 525 S FM Rd. 2818, 822-4897.

True Vine Missionary Baptist, 807 W. 22nd. 775-5395.

United Free Will Baptist, 3707 N. East Bypass, 778-0063.

United Missionary Baptist, 1600 M L King W. 775-7729.

Wellborn Baptist, 3991 McCullough Rd. 690-2360.

Bible

Grace Bible, 701 Anderson, 693-2911.

Brethren

Brethren of Bryan-College Station, 2650 Hwy. 6 S. 693-3606.

Catholic

Catholicism came to Texas with the Spanish explorers. The first diocese was established in 1841 and has since become one of the leading religions in the state.

St. Anthony's Catholic, 301 W. 29th. 822-5224. MDO

St. Anthony's Catholic, 306 S. Parker Ave. 823-8145.

St. Joseph Catholic, 600 E. 26th. 822-2721.

St. Mary's Catholic Center, 103 Nagle, 846-5717.

St. Thomas Aquinas Catholic, 2541 Hwy. 6 S. 693-6994.

Santa Teresa Catholic, 1212 Lucky St. 822-2932.

Christian Disciples of Christ

The Christian or Disciples of Christ movement began in Texas in 1841. Controversy arose over home mission work and the use of instrumental music in services. As a result, the religion split into the Disciples of Christ and the Church of Christ.

First Christian of Bryan-College Station, 900 S. Ennis, 823-5451.

Christian-Independent

Central Christian, 3205 Lakeview, 823-5747.

Christian Science

The Christian Science movement spread into Austin in 1889. Christian Science churches are characterized by their operation of free reading rooms for the distribution of literature.

Christian Science Society & Reading Room, 201 Boyett St. 846-4082.

Church of Christ

The Church of Christ formed as a result of the Disciples of Christ dispute over home missions and the use of instrumental music during services.

A&M Church of Christ, 1001 FM Rd. 2818, 693-0400. PS

Benchley Church of Christ, 1101 W. OSR, 778-0608.

Cavitt Church of Christ, 3200 Cavitt Ave. 822-4844.

Church of Christ Central, 1600 E. 29th. 822-3010.

Martin Luther King Jr. Street Church of Christ, 1104 M L King E. 822-7790.

Twin City Church of Christ, 810 E. Southwest Pkwy. 693-1758.

Church of God in Christ

Lily of the Valley Church of God in Christ, 606 N. Reed Ave. 822-2096.

The Savior's Temple, 5002 W. 28th St. 779-1059.

Church of Jesus Christ of Latter-Day Saints

Church of Jesus Christ of Latter-Day Saints, 2500 Barak Ln. 846-3516.

The Church of Jesus Christ of Latter-Day Saints, 401 Anderson, 695-7021.

Congregational

The Congregational movement surfaced after the Civil War. In 1906, the church split with one group joining the Presbyterians and the other affiliating with the Disciples of Christ.

Friends Congregational, 2200 Southwood Dr. 693-7021.

Ecumenical

United Campus Ministry, 301 Church Ave. 846-1221.

Episcopal

In 1883, R.M. Chapman of New York was sent as an Episcopalian missionary to Texas. In 1849, The Protestant Episcopal Diocese of Texas was established at Matagorda.

Episcopal Student Center, 902 George Bush Dr. 693-4245.

St. Andrew's Episcopal, 217 W. 26th. 822-5176.

St. Francis Episcopal, 1101 Rock Prairie Rd. 696-1491.

St. Thomas' Episcopal, 906 George Bush Dr. 696-1726.

Evangelical Covenant

Brazos Community Evangelical Church, P.O. Box 10130, College Station (holds services at alternative sites), 260-1922.

Evangelical Free

Hope Evangelical Free, FM Rd. 60, 846-2382.

Full Gospel

Assemblage of Praise, 900 E. 29th St. 779-6316.

Covenant Family, 4010 Harvey Rd. 774-1269.

New Life In Christ, 401 Lawrence, 779-1682.

Interdenominational

Hosanna Christian Fellowship, 3141 Briarcrest Dr. 776-1938.

Jewish

Jewish families were among the "First Three Hundred" in Stephen Austin's original Texas settlements.

Congregation Beth Shalom, 101 N. Coulter Dr. 822-2738.

> **FYI**
> The Brazos Valley Cowboy Church holds services every Sunday at 10 a.m.. at the Brazos Valley Auction Barnes on Hwy. 21. This down-home church is non-denominational and welcomes everyone. Call Pastor Jeff Young (589-1215) for more information.

Lutheran

Beautiful Savior, 1007 Krenek Tap Rd. 693-4514.

Bethel Lutheran, 410 Bethel Ln. 822-2742.

Holly Cross Lutheran, 1200 Foxfire Dr. 764-3992.

Our Savior's Lutheran, 315 Tauber, 846-5011.

Peace Lutheran, 2201 Rio Grande Blvd. 693-4403.

University Lutheran Chapel & Student Center, 315 College Main, 846-6687.

Metaphysical Christianity

Healing Light Center, 1808 Brothers Blvd. 694-1838.

Methodist

The Methodist movement came to Texas in 1814 with William Stevenson, one of the earliest Protestant ministers to preach in the state.

Christ United, 1902 Pinon Dr. 696-4673.

First United, 506 E. 28th. 779-1324.

United Methodist

A&M United, 417 W. University Dr. 846-8731. PS & MDO

Aldersgate, 2201 E. Hwy 6 Bypass, 696-1376.

Christ United Methodist, Meeting at College Station Junior High. 690-4673 (Beginning Nov. 1' 1998 at new facility at 4203 State Highway. 6 S.).

First United, 506 E. 28th. 779-1324.

Iglesia Methodista Unida, 2506 Cavitt Ave. 823-7947.

Lee Chapel, 903 N. Washington Ave. 822-0437.

St. Paul's United, 2506 Cavitt Ave. 779-7608.

Wesley Foundation-Methodist Student Center, 201 Tauber St. 846-4701.

Nazarene

In Texas, the Church of the Nazarene was formed in 1898 from the Church of Christ.

Church of the Nazarene, 2122 Wm Joel Bryan Pkwy. 776-2735.

Non-Denominational

Bible Way Full Gospel, 1406 Ursuline Ave. 822-7797.

Bryan First Church of God, 2002 E. Hwy 21, 778-7680.

Covenant Family, 4010 Harvey Rd. 774-1269.

Fellowship Community, 1700 Kyle Ave. S. 764-8776.

Grace Bible, 701 Anderson, 693-2911.

Pentecostal

Endtime Evangelistic Pentecostal, 504 M L King W. 775-1595.

New Life Tabernacle, 6083 E. Hwy 21, 778-1539.

United Pentecostal, 2206 E Hwy 21, 778-1806.

Presbyterian

Presbyterian mission work began in Texas in 1837 under the patronage of the Synod of Mississippi. In 1840, a Presbyteria was established and in 1851 the Synod of Texas came into being.

A&M Presbyterian, 301 Church Ave. 846-5631. PS & MDO

First Presbyterian, 1100 Carter Creek Pkwy. 823-8073.

Photo: First United Methodist Church in Bryan
First United Methodist Church is Bryan's oldest Methodist Congregation. The first church building was completed in 1869.

Trinity Presbyterian meets at Pebble Creek Elementary School, Office 208B SW Pkwy E. 694-7700.

Westminster Presbyterian, 3333 Oak Ridge Dr. 776-1185.

Seventh Day Adventist

The Adventist movement came to Texas in the later part of the 1880s. Adventists are characterized by their recognition of Saturday as the Sabbath.

Seventh Day Adventist, 1218 Ettle, 822-2995.

Unitarian

Unitarian Fellowship, 305 Wellborn Rd. 696-5285.

United Church of Christ

Faith United Church of Christ, 2402 S. College Ave. 823-0135.

Friends Congregational Church, 2200 Southwood Dr. 683-7021.

Rent to Rent

The secret is out …Bryan-College Station is a great place to live, work, study and retire. It is both the quality of life and the opportunities that abound here which attract so many new residents.

The air is clean, the schools are excellent and our neighborhoods are safe. We have a growing economy, low unemployment and affordable housing. For as little as $250, newcomers can rent a little piece of Aggieland to call their own!

Condominiums, duplexes, townhouses and single family homes come in all sizes, styles and rental price ranges. Due to space and time considerations, none of these types of rental properties are included in this chapter. Try *The Eagle* newspaper or one of several locator services to find out what is currently available in these categories. This chapter focuses on apartments that are available as efficiencies or with one to five bedroom floor plans.

In recent years, the list of amenities included in apartment rent has gone far beyond a dishwasher, microwave and washer/dryer set. There is an amazing assortment of options available today.

Internet access, fax and copy machines, warehouse storage, roommate matching, ice makers, club rooms, individual leases and free video libraries are just some of the perks available to apartment dwellers. New amenities are added frequently while unpopular services are abandoned. Additionally, some apartment complexes cover the water, sewer and garbage expenses under the terms of the lease. Even electric, cable or other premium services are sometimes included in the rental price. With so many options it is difficult to know where to begin!

To make the task of finding an apartment more manageable, it might make sense to determine a housing budget, find the apartments that fall into your "affordable" category and then compare the amenities and terms of the lease. Keep in mind that most apartment complexes require a signed lease and minimum deposit to cover any future cleaning fees or damages.

Apartments are available for rent throughout the year but as might be expected, August is a busy month with the students coming back for fall term. The starting rent depends upon the location, size and the amenities that come with the apartment. The following price codes are based upon the apartment complex's published minimum starting rents and when possible, the minimum

---

Apartment Price Codes

$ - $200 - $300	$$$- $401 to $500
$$ - $300 - $400	$$$$- $501+

---

lease period. Call the apartment complexes that you are interested in for the terms of the lease and a current list of amenities.

$$ Academic Village Apartments 3914 Old College Rd. (B) 846-9196 (12 months).

$$ Allendale Apartments 3130 E. Villa Maria, (B) 776-6760 (1 year).

$$ Arbor Square 1700 Southwest Parkway (CS) 693-3701.

$$$$ The Arbors at Wolf Pen Creek 301 Holleman E. (CS) 694-5100 (1 year).

$$$$ Aurora Gardens Apartments Aurora Court (CS) 696-3095 (9 months).

$$ Balcones Apartments 1000 Balcones (CS) 268-8620 (1 year).

$$$ Brookside Apartments 1525 E. 29th St. (B) 775-6777 (6 months).

$$$$ Brownstone Apartments 603 Southwest Parkway (CS) 696-9771.

$$$ Brookwood Apartments 1601 Valley View (CS) 260-9611 (9 months).

$$ Casa Blanca 4110 College Main (B) 846-1413 (1 year).

$$ Casa Del Sol 401 Stasney (CS) 696-3455 (summer).

$$$$ Casa Verde 700 San Pedro (CS) 268-8620 (9 months).

$$$ College Court Apartments 3300 S. College (B) 823-7039 (9 ½ months).

$$ College Main Apartments 4302 College Main (B) 846-2089 (12 months).

$$$ The Colony 1101 Southwest Parkway (CS) 693-0804 (12 months).

$$$$ College Park Enclave 1800 Holleman (CS) 694-3700 (9 months).

$$$$ College Park Ridge 2250 Dartmouth (CS) 694-4100 (12 months).

$$$ College Park-Treehouse, L.P. 800 Marion Pugh (CS) 764-8892 (12 months).

$$ Country Place Apartments 3902 College Main (B) 691-6200.

$$ Doux Chene Apartments 1401 FM 2818 (CS) 693-1906 (9 months).

$$$ Eastmark Apartments 7600 Central Park Lane (CS) 693-8066 (1 month).

$$$ Forest Creek Apartments 1005 Varde (B) 779-3637 (12 months).

$$ Forest Knoll 2700 Evergreen (B) 268-8620 (9 months).

$$$ French Quarter Apartments 601 N. Cross (CS) 846-8981 (12 months).

$$ The Gables 401 University Oaks (CS) 693-1188 (9 months).

$$$ Huntington 1907 Dartmouth (CS) 693-8922 (9 months).

$$ Kensington Place 401 Harvey Road (CS) 693-1111 (3 months).

$ Koenig Lane Apartments 111 Koenig Lane (B) 822-2191 1 year

$$ The Landing 3200 Finfeather (B) 822-7321 (6 months).

$$ Lincoln Square Apartments 313 Lincoln Street (CS) 693-2720.

$$$ Meadowland Apartments 410 South Texas (CS) (9 months).

$$ Melrose 601 Luther St. West (CS) 693-9432 (1 year).

$$ Meridian 306 Redmond (CS) 696-3177 (9 months).

$$ Monterrey 2000 Kazmeier (B) 268-0840 (summer).

$$ Natalie Apartments 807 Natalie (B) 268-8620 (1 year).

FYI

Some apartments include utilities, cable TV or other amenities in the rent. Verify what is included for an accurate comparison.

$$$$ The Oaks of Villa Maria 1305 W. Villa Maria (B) 823-2232 (9 months).

$$$ Oakwood Apartments 503 Southwest Parkway (CS) 696-9100.

$$$ The Oaks Apartments 3301 Providence Ave. (B) 822-7650.

$$$ Parkway Apartments 1600 Southwest Parkway (CS) 693-6540 (9 months).

$$$$ Parkway Circle 401 Southwest Parkway (CS) 696-6909 (9 months).

$$$ Pepper Tree Apartments 2701 Longmire (CS) 693-5731.

$ Plantation Oaks 1501 Harvey Rd. (CS) 693-1110.

$$$ Redstone Apartments 1301 Barthelow (CS) 696-1848 (9 months).

$$$$ Saddlewood Apartment Homes 3625 Wellborn Rd. (B) 846-5601.

$$$ Scandia 401 Anderson St. (CS) 693-6505 (9 months).

$$ Scholar's Inn 401 Cooner St. (CS) 846-9196 (1 year).

$$ Sevilla Apartments 1501 Holleman (CS) 693-2108 (9 months).

$$$ Sonnenblick Apartments 3700 Plainsman (B) 260-8090 (9 ½ months).

$$ Sterling University 117 Holleman Drive W. (CS) 696-5711 (1 year).

$$ Stonewood Village 1903 Dartmouth (CS) 693-0077 (9 months).

$$$ Treehouse II Apartments 400 Marion Pugh (CS) 696-7871 (9 months).

$$ University Acres 3180 Cain Road (CS) 268-8620 (1 year).

$$ University Terrace 1700 George Bush (CS) 693-1930 (6 months).

$$$ Valley View 2601 Pecan Knoll (B) 268-8620 (1 year).

$$ Villa Oaks West 1107 Verde (B) 779-1136.

$ Villa West Apartments 3500 Finfeather (B) 822-7772.

$$ Willow Oaks 3902 East 29th St. (B) 846-7996 (6 months).

$$$ Windhill/Sunset Apartments 2301 Broadmoor (B) 776-7094.

$$$$ Walden Pond 700 FM 2818 (CS) 696-5777 (9 months).

$ Willowick 502 Southwest Parkway (CS) 693-1325 (summer).

Photo: Saddlewood Apartment Homes
Saddlewood, like many apartment s offer amenities such as swimming pools, video libraries and tennis courts

◆◆◆◆◆◆◆
Bryan-College Station

is a home rule community with both cities operating under a council/manager system of government.

Media Moguls

If you're looking for the lowdown on news and events in Bryan-College Station, look no further. Radio Stations, newspapers, magazines and a local television station cover what's happening and why.

Here is a rundown on some of the media options that will keep residents and visitors abreast of local, regional, national and international happenings.

Newspapers

A-Thrifty Nickel

A weekly publication designed to bring buyers and sellers together. Everything from air conditioners to wanted items is included. Also, adoption services, employment and work-for-hire situations are listed. Thurs. is the publication day. Distributed free at area restaurants and stores. 923 S. Texas Ave. (B) 822-7899.

The Battalion

The 104 year old official student newspaper on the Texas A&M Campus. Published daily except Sat. & Sun. Covers campus and national news and sports. Distributed free on campus or at a subscription rate of $60 per school year, $30 for the fall or spring semester and $17.50 for the summer. 203 Reed McDonald Building, Texas A&M Campus (CS) 845-3313.

Bryan-College Station Eagle

Bryan-College Station's only daily newspaper has grown and become more diverse over the past few years. The *Eagle* covers local, regional and national events, news, sports and business. The *Eagle's* specialty publications such as Brazos *Valley Real Estate Magazine, The Golden Eagle* and the *Senior Resource Book* fill a wide variety of community's informational needs. The newsstand price is $.50 daily except on Sundays which is $1.25. Available at area stores, restaurants, motels and via home delivery. 1729 Briarcrest, (B) 776-4444.

The Guide

This monthly is the new kid on the newsstand, covering the entertainment scene in Bryan-College Station. Includes local events, places of worship, music and restaurants. Distributed free at area restaurants and shops. 1511 Texas Ave. S., Suite 139 (CS) 764-8989.

The Press

A weekly publication covering local entertainment and happenings. Supplemental information includes Antique Talk, MatchMaker, and Soap Opera Updates. Publication day is Thurs. Distributed free at area businesses with limited local delivery. 725 E. Villa Maria Rd. (B) 823-0088.

> ## FYI
> Check out these local publications to find out what's going on in Bryan-College Station.

Magazines

Etc.

This monthly features profiles of people and places in Bryan-College Station and includes one of the best current event listings in town. Distributed free at area businesses. 7607 Eastmark Dr. Suite 250-C (CS) 693-6235.

Insite

Bryan-College Station's own city magazine covers people, places and trends that are important to residents of the twin cities. The newsstand price is $1.95. Available at local stores. 123 W. Wm. Joel Pkwy (B) 823-5567.

La Voz Hispana

This monthly magazine is published in Spanish covering music, events and people in the Hispanic Community. Distributed free at dozens of area businesses. P.O. Box 1774 (B) 822-0503.

Radio Stations
Contemporary and Rock

KTAM 1240 AM

Adult Contemporary. 1240 Villa Maria (B) 776-1240.

KTSR 92.1 FM

Album Rock. 2700 E. Bypass (CS) 846-1150.

KHLR 103.9 FM

Rock. 1240 Villa Maria (B) 776-1240.

KKYS MIX 104.7 FM

Hits of the 70s, 80s, and 90s. 1730 Briarcrest Dr. (B) 846-KKYS.

KZTR 101.9 FM

Classic rock. 1200 Briarcrest Dr. (B) 268-3100.

Christian

KAGG 1510 AM

Contemporary Christian. 202 Carson (B) 779-1510.

Country

KORA 98.3 FM

Counrty. 1240 Villa Maria Rd. (B) 776-1240.

Aggle 96 96.1 FM

Country. 1730 Briarcrest (B) 268-9696.

Public and Talk

KEOS 89.1FM

Public Radio, enjoyable and eclectic. 508 E. 32nd. (B) 779-5367.

KAMU 90.9 FM

National Public Radio affiliate. Moore Communications Center, Texas A&M campus 845-5613.

WTAW 1150 AM

News, Sports and Weather 2700 E. Bypass (CS) 846-1150.

Television Stations

KBTX Channel 3

CBS affiliate. 4141 E. 29th St. (B) 846-7777.

Brazos County

includes prime farmland that covers between 11-20% of the county's total acreage.

Big Business

The American Dream – a decent home, a car and enough money to educate the kids – begins with a job. In Bryan-College Station, we are fortunate to have a diverse and growing economic base that provides employment opportunities in business, industry and government.

The largest percentage of workers in Bryan-College Station are employed by the state. According to the Texas Workforce Commission's 1996 report, some 19,300 Bryan-College Station employees labored for the Lone Star State. The majority were on Texas A&M's payroll as faculty and staff. The service category, which covers everything from restaurants to auto-shops, was the second largest employment sector with some 13,500 workers. The third largest employment category was retail trade with 12,800 employees. Local government, manufacturing and construction were also among the largest employment categories.

Although the number of small businesses (those with less than 50 employees) dominate our commercial landscape, it tends to be the giants, which are initially sought out for potential employment, sales opportunities and curiosity.

To aid readers in this endeavor, we have provided a list of some of the largest employers in the twin cities along with addresses, telephone numbers and the approximate number of employees. Individual names are not provided because almost as soon as they hit the printed page, many would be out-of-date.

If you're applying for a job, call the company and ask who is in charge of personnel. If you are making sales calls, contact the person holding the appropriate title for the type of product that you sell. In any case, be sure to confirm the mailing or street address before sending literature or making a trip to the business site – companies do relocate!

Alenco/Reliant Building Products
Window and door manufacturing
950 employees
615 West Carson Street
Bryan, TX 77801-1199
779-7770
FAX 822-3259

Anco Insurance
Consumer insurance
130 employees
1733 Briarcrest
Bryan, TX 77802-2793
776-2626
FAX 776-1308

Blinn College
Education
293 employees
2520 Villa Maria Rd.
P.O. Box 6030
Bryan, TX 77805-6030
821-0200
FAX 821-0249

BJ Services
Oil field, cement and fracturing
company
150 employees
1680 Independence Ave.
Bryan, TX 77803-2003
779-8125
FAX 779-3892

Brazos County
County government
796 employees
300 E. 26th St.
Ste. 114
Bryan, TX 77803-5363
361-4102

Brazos Sportswear
Custom shirt printing
150 employees
114 Holleman Drive
College Station, TX 77840-4235
693-9664
FAX 693-2032

Britt Rice Electric
Electrical Equipment
285 employees
3002-D Longmire
P.O. Box 10477
College Station, TX 77842
693-4076
FAX 693-9785

Bryan (City of)
City government
859 employees
P.O. Box 1000
Bryan, TX 77805-1000
361-3600

FAX 361-3702

Bryan Independent School District
Education
1,868 employees
101 N. Texas Ave.
Bryan, TX 77805-6030
821-5202
FAX 823-0352

Bryan Coca-Cola Bottling Co.
Beverages
125 employees
201 East 24th Street
P.O. Drawer 433
Bryan, TX 77806
823-8153
FAX 821-3244

Bryan-College Station Eagle
Newspaper
150 employees
1729 Briarcrest Drive
Bryan, Texas 77802
776-4444
FAX 774-0496

Bryan Dr. Pepper Bottling Company
Beverages
120 employees
201 East 24th Street
Bryan, TX 77806
822-2032
FAX 821-3244

Bryan Tank
Farm machinery
130 employees
4400 East Highway 21
Bryan, TX 77808
778-0034
FAX 778-0615

See "Just the Facts"
p. 106

101

Business & Personal

In Manor East Mall
Suite 302

P.O. Box 3043
Bryan, Texas 77805-3043
409-822-1040
Fax 409-775-4252
E-Mail blb@txcyber.com

Bryan Utilities
Electrical utility
193 employees
205 East 28th Street
P.O. Box 1000
Bryan, TX 77805
821-5750
FAX 821-5795

CIC Corporation
Insurance
130 employees
200 Greens Prairie Road
College Station, TX 77845-9394
690-5208
FAX 690-5408

College Station (City of)
City government
636 employees
1101 Texas Ave. South
P.O. Box 9960
College Station, TX 77842-7960
764-3510

College Station Independent School District
Education
800 employees
1812 Welsh Ave.
College Station, TX 77840-4800
764-5455
FAX 764-5492

College Station Medical Center
Hospital
400 employees
1604 Rock Prairie Road
P.O. ox 10000
College Station, TX 77842-3500
764-5100
FAX 696-7373

Dawson Well Solutions, L.C.
Equipment Rental
200 employees
6115 Hwy 21 East
Bryan, TX 77803
778-1800
FAX 778-0847

Econophone, Inc.
Telephone systems and services
110 employees
3833 S. Texas Ave.
Suites 130 & 240
Bryan, TX 77802-4015
260-0063
FAX 260-1244

First American Bank SSB
Financial institution
300 employees
1111 Briarcrest Drive
P.O. Box 1033
Bryan, TX 77805-1033
268-7575

GTE
Telephone systems and services
154 employees
300 Holleman Drive East
College Station, TX 77840
694-4787

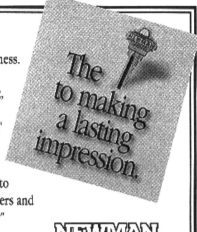
Gooseneck Trailer MFG. Inc.
Farm machinery
140 employees
4400 East Hwy 21
P.O. Box 832
Bryan, TX 77806
778-0034
FAX 778-0615

Insurance Information Exchange
Software development for the
insurance industry
300 employees
3001 East Bypass
College Station, TX 77845
693-6122

Kent Moore Cabinets, Inc.
Cabinet manufacturing
188 employees
1460 Fountain Avenue

Bryan, TX 77801-1129
775-2906
FAX 775-0591

Knowledge Based Systems, Inc.
Computer programming/systems
100 employees
1500 University Drive East
College Station, TX 77840
260-5274
FAX 260-1965

Lowe's Home Improvement Warehouse
Retail
150 employees
3225 Freedom Boulevard
Bryan, TX 77802
774-4141
FAX 774-4340

New South/West Baking Company
Food
175 employees
600 Phil Gramm Blvd.
Bryan, TX 77807
778-3502

Northrop Grumman
Electronic component manufacturing
134 employees
2501 East Bypass
College Station, TX 77845
764-2200

O I Corporation
Testing and measurement instruments
145 employees
151 Graham Road
P.O. Box 690-1711
FAX 690-0440

St. Joseph Regional Health Center
Hospital
1,170 employees
2801 Franciscan St.

Bryan, TX 7702-2544
776-2446
FAX 774-4590

Sanderson Farms Inc.
Poultry production
600 employees
2000 Shiloh Ave.
Bryan, TX 77803
361-3410
FAX 361-3422

Scott and White Clinic
Healthcare
375 employees
1600 University Drive E.
College Station, TX 77840-2642
691-3300
FAX 268-3658

See "Media Moguls"
p. 98

Southcorp Packaging USA, Inc.
Rubber and plastic products
125 employees
1100 North FM 2818
Bryan, TX 77803-1182
821-2304
FAX 361-0343

Target
Retail
200 employees
2100 Texas Ave. S.
College Station, TX 77840-3918
693-8400

Texas A&M University and System
Education
19,971 employees
TAMU Office Of the President
College Station, TX 77843-1246
845-2217
FAX 845-5027

Texas Digital Systems, Inc.
Digital signs
100 employees
512 West Loop FM 2818
College Station, TX 77845
693-9378
FAX 764-8650

Texas Municipal Power Agency
Electrical services
137 employees
P.O. Box 7000

Bryan, TX 77805
873-1130
FAX 873-1186

Universal Computer Systems
Computer programming/systems
200+ employees
700 East University Drive
Suite 115
College Station, TX 77840
846-8111
FAX 691-2743

Wal-Mart
Retail
200 employees
1815 Brothers Blvd.
College Station, TX 77845-5413
693-3095

Wal-Mart Supercenter
Retail
600 employees
2200 Briarcrest Dr.
Bryan, TX 77802-5000
776-6441

Young Brothers Contractors, Inc.
Highway and street construction
300 employees
7601 West Hwy 21
Bryan, TX 77807
779-1112
FAX 823-2797

Photo: Rhonda Brinkmann
St. Joseph Regional Health Center employees some 1,170 workers

Just the Facts

In 1996, Bryan-College Station was named the fastest growing U.S. metropolitan area in terms of household growth by the *Wall Street Journal*. One year later, the twin cities were named the fifth fastest growing metropolitan area in the United States by *Kiplinger's Personal Finance*. In the 1997-1998 *American Almanac of Jobs and Salaries*, Bryan-College Station was touted as the third fastest growing U.S. metropolitan area in terms of new job growth for the years 1995 to 2025. How are these determinations made? They are all based on demographics and other statistics that are collected by local, state and federal agencies.

Sometimes, as is the case with the data in this chapter, a private company will update and project the governmental data beyond its' original collection date, in order to reflect recent trends.

Demographics paint a numerical picture of the population. The data reveal the ethnic make-up, the average age, the median income and more about a specific population. Such information is more than merely interesting, it can be quite useful.

Demographics help businesses to estimate sales potential, identify growth areas and to analyze customer needs. Demographics tell us when to build more churches, schools and shopping malls. Demographics can surprise us by telling us things that we may not know about the city in which we live.

The tables that follow can help explain the similarities and the differences between Bryan and College Station, and show how the twin cities compare to the rest of the state.

> **Claritas Inc.**, a pioneer in the consumer information industry provided the data used in this chapter. By press time, the company will have data available for 1998 and 2000. Call Claritas at 1-800-780-4237 for all your information needs.

Population

Attribute	Texas	Bryan	College Station
2002 Total	21032734	64078	61428
1997 Total	19384454	60971	58351
1990 Total	16986510	55002	52487
1980 Total	14229189	48062	38130
% Change 90-97	14.1	10.9	11.2
% Change 80-90	19.4	14.4	37.7

Total Households

Attribute	Texas	Bryan	College Station
2002 Total	7530871	24333	21347
1997 Total	6912143	23070	20081
1990 Total	6070937	20741	17722
1980 Total	4929234	17530	12216
% Change 90-97	13.9	11.2	13.3
% Change 80-90	23.2	18.3	45.1

Average Household Size

Year	Texas	Bryan	College Station
2002	2.74	2.59	2.35
1997	2.74	2.60	2.35
1997	2.73	2.61	2.33

Bryan-College Station

is one of the least expensive cities in the United States to live and the third most affordable place to live in Texas.

American Chamber of Commerce Researchers Association

Total Families

Attribute	Texas	Bryan	College Station
2002	5303516	15438	9273
1997	4900921	14739	8760
1990	4343878	13358	7741
% Change 90-97	12.8	10.3	13.2

Population by Race and Hispanic Origin

Attribute	Texas	%	Bryan	%	College Station	%
Total Population	19384454	%	60970	%	58351	%
White (non-Hispanic)	11098759	57.3	35825	58.8	43168	74.0
Black (non-Hispanic)	2269241	11.7	10061	16.5	4286	7.3
Asian (non-Hispanic)	453653	2.3	1287	2.1	4392	7.5
All Other (non-Hispanic)	90337	0.5	196	0.3	177	0.3
Hispanic Origin	5472481	28.2	13601	22.3	6328	10.8

Photo: City of Bryan
Neighbors working together

1997 Population by Age

Attribute	Texas	%	Bryan	%	College Station	%
Total Population	19384454	%	60971	%	58351	%
<5	1551623	8.0	5107	8.4	2651	4.5
5-9	1555655	8.0	4990	8.2	2692	4.6
10-14	1496990	7.7	4646	7.6	2473	4.2
15-19	1422108	7.3	3999	6.6	9630	16.5
20-24	1318448	6.8	6177	10.1	17509	30.0
25-29	1544007	8.0	5564	9.1	4804	8.2
30-34	1533986	7.9	5148	8.4	4180	7.2
35-39	1597294	8.2	5043	8.3	3643	6.2
40-44	1484317	7.7	4383	7.2	2859	4.9
45-54	2285401	11.8	6038	9.9	3747	6.4
55-64	1479720	7.6	3849	6.3	1991	3.4
65-74	1167543	6.0	3045	5.0	1145	2.0
75-84	693533	3.6	2099	3.4	739	1.3
85+	253828	1.3	888	1.5	280	0.5
Total Median Age (in years)	32.6	-	30.0	-	22.4	-

Per capita Income

Attribute	Texas	Bryan	College Station
1997	$17317	$16744	$13258
1989 (Census)	$12884	$11966	$9074
% Change 89-97	34.4	39.9	46.1

Median Household Income

Attribute	Texas	Bryan	College Station
1997	$34123	$29836	$21428
1989 (Census)	$27058	$22444	$15121
% Change 89-97	26.1	32.9	41.7

Median Family Household Income

Attribute	Texas	Bryan	College Station
1997	$40767	$39187	$46138
1989 (Census)	$32143	$30133	$33485
% Change 89-97	26.8	30.0	37.8

1997 Assets Minus Liabilities (Household Wealth)

Attribute	Texas	Bryan	College Station
Average Household Wealth	$122033	$100646	$62599
Median Household Wealth	$49707	$24453	$11231

Age, race, gender, wealth and other demographics are indicative of the way that we spend our money. For example, College Station residents spend far less than the national average on floor coverings. Why? Because the majority of the city's young population (the Median age in College Station is 22.4 compared to 32.6 for Texas) are not homeowners.

In the 1990 Census it was reported that only 23.1% of College Station's housing units were owner-occupied compared to the state total of 52.7% - a whopping 66.8% were occupied by renters. It's no wonder that College Station's average expenditures on floor coverings are less. The 1990 figures show that the percent of owner-occupied housing units for the state was 52.7% - more than twice that of College Station.

Claritas, Inc. provided the consumer spending data that follows. The data is based upon the Bureau of Labor Statistics Consumer Expenditure Survey and updated through a proprietary methodology.

All data is indexed against an average U.S. expenditure of 100. An Index of 100 means that the expenditures are at the national average while an index of 107 is somewhat above the national average. Likewise, an index of 98 is just below the national average.

1997 Expenditures by Selected Product Categories
(Thousands of dollars/Index)

Product Category	Texas		Bryan		College Station	
Food at Home	26612168	96	82329	89	62560	77
Food Away from Home	17573421	97	56164	93	46594	89
Alcoholic Beverages at Home	1682242	98	5736	100	5200	104
Alcoholic Beverages Away from Home	1038801	88	3592	92	3652	107
Women's Apparel	5179826	91	16030	85	12941	79
Men's Apparel	2969334	92	9260	86	8057	86
Furniture	3554333	96	11163	90	9254	86
Major Appliances	1443113	96	4354	87	3252	74
Small Appliances & Housewares	892148	95	2759	88	2236	82
TV, Radio & Sound Equipment	4842171	97	15483	93	13461	93
Transportation	49769791	100	157159	95	136156	94

Photos: Rhonda Brinkmann

Age and income influence a consumer's buying decisions

Index